HANDBOOK OF THE
BLACK ARTS

D1494243

HANDBOOK OF THE
BLACK ARTS

J. W. WICKWAR

SENATE

Handbook of the Black Arts

First published in 1925 as *Witchcraft and the Black Art* by
Herbert Jenkins Ltd, London

This edition first published in 1996 by Senate, an imprint of
Random House UK Ltd, Random House, 20 Vauxhall Bridge
Road, London SW1V 2SA

Copyright © John William Wickwar 1925

This publication may not be reproduced, stored in a retrieval
system or transmitted, in any form or by any means, electronic,
mechanical, photocopying or otherwise, without the prior
written permission of the publishers.

ISBN 1 85958 164 1

Printed and bound in Guernsey by The Guernsey Press Co. Ltd

Dedicated

TO THE MEMORY OF

W. H. R. RIVERS

M.D., D.Sc., LL.D., F.R.S.,

WHOSE FRIENDSHIP AS

PRESIDENT OF THE FOLKLORE SOCIETY

IS COUNTED AMONG THE AUTHOR'S

MOST TREASURED POSSESSIONS

FOREWORD

THE old craft of the witches, like many a craft since, was a close order ; its members were sworn to secrecy. This being so, it kept such records as it made in safe keeping, and although at one time or another there must have been many of them in existence—for every district had its Coven and its Register of Adherents—there is probably to-day not a single one in any library the wide world o'er. In early ecclesiastic and in mediæval literature, however, references to witchcraft are numerous, and it is from a study of these that we are able to form an opinion as to what witchcraft really was.

In the pages that follow, an endeavour has been made to set out in an interesting manner the story of the craft from earliest times.

As, up to the present, very little of a popular nature has been written on the subject, it has been thought that such an account as is here given may be appreciated by the general reading public.

CONTENTS

THE WITCH

" Within a gloomy dimble she doth dwell,
Down in a pit o'ergrown with brakes and briers,
Close by the ruins of a shaken abbey,
Torn with an earthquake down into the ground,—
'Mongst graves and grots, near an old charnel house,
Where you shall find her sitting in her form
As fearful and melancholic as that
She is about, with caterpillars' kells
And knotty cobwebs rounded in with spells.
Then she steals forth to make ewes
Cast their lambs, swine eat their farrow,
And housewife's tun not work, nor the milk churn !
Writhe children's wrists and suck their breath in sleep,
Get vials of their blood ! and where the sea
Cast up his slimy ooze, search for a weed
To open locks with, and to rivet charms
Planted about her in the wicked feat
Of all her mischiefs, which are manifold."

Ben Jonson.

WITCHCRAFT AND THE BLACK ART

CHAPTER I

WITCHCRAFT : A PRIMITIVE CULT

" What are these
So wither'd, and so wild in their attire,
That look not like the inhabitants o' the earth,
And yet are on't ? "

BANQUO.

IN order that the reader may understand aright the inner meaning of the many strange narratives recorded in the following pages, it will be necessary here at the opening to explain just who the witches were and what witchcraft really was. Let it be said, however, that knowing how disliked preliminaries usually are, and especially when of an explanatory nature, this shall be done in as brief a manner as possible.

Although some authorities on witchcraft write as though it was a product of the sixteenth century, there can be no doubt but that it was firmly established more than a dozen centuries earlier, when paganism first gave place to Christianity. Certain it is also that before witchcraft became a kind of rubbish heap for worn-out creeds and superstitions which were made bad use of in times of social unrest, political change, and religious schism, it was essentially—for the want of a better descriptive term—a religious organisation ; crude, it may be, but with principles nevertheless, and a belief that called for adoration, sacrifice, and service. Moreover, it was presided over by a priestly craft who held their position on sufferance, according to the amount of magical or mystical power imputed to them.

Witchcraft, therefore, being a pseudo-religious organisation, was not without its recognised observances, which, doubtless, had evolved from immemorial belief in magic as a set-off against the mysteries of Nature.

These observances, fundamental in themselves, changed with the periods through which they passed, and adapted themselves to whatever the popular fancy or the prevailing fashion happened to be. Thus, whereas the ritual of the witches before the fourth century was essentially pagan in character, it was for some centuries after both pagan and Christian.

The reason for such a contradictory combination may be found in the fact that the early converts from the old stock, including as they did those that practised witchcraft, did not renounce all the ritual they had been accustomed to observe at the same time that they changed their gods.

Those under whose authority and guidance the conversion of Britain was taking place knew this, and understood human nature only too well, with its vain hankerings after mere formalities, than to have expected anything else, and they were also well aware that the visible symbolic form of a religion always takes a firmer hold of the imagination than mere belief.

In addition, St. Augustine knew that if the conversion of England was to be carried through to a successful conclusion he dare not interfere too much with what had until then been the custom of his unruly neophytes ; in fact, he harmonised as far as he thought he safely could his own customs with theirs. Pagan temples were changed into churches by the mere sprinkling of holy water so that the converts would not have to grow accustomed to a new environment, and the sacrifices that previously had been made to heathen gods were replaced by processions in honour of some saint or martyr ; while oxen were slaughtered, not to propitiate idols, but in praise of the true God, knowledge of whom had been brought to them.

A letter from Pope Gregory the Great, in the sixth century, to Abbot Mellitus, then going to Britain, desires him to tell Augustine, the first Archbishop of Canterbury, that "after mature deliberation on the affair of the English" he was "of the opinion that the temples of the idols in that nation ought not to be destroyed, but that the idols should." He further orders the temples to be sprinkled with holy water, and relics to be placed in them ; and because our ancestors sacrificed oxen in their pagan worship, he advises that the objects of the sacrifice be exchanged ; and permits them to build huts of the boughs of trees about the temples so transformed into churches ; and on the day of the dedication, or nativities of the martyrs whose relics they contain, to kill the cattle, and celebrate the solemnity with religious feasting. (Bede's *Eccl. Hist. of Eng.*)

So persistently were the deliberations of

Pope Gregory adhered to, that in the metropolis itself, hundreds of years afterwards, it was usual to bring up a fat buck to the altar of old St. Paul's, with horns blowing, in the middle of the service. For on the spot where old St. Paul's stood, or very near it, there was once according to tradition a temple of Diana.

That pagan temples could have been so easily changed into Christian churches is of course a striking tribute to the adaptability of the English temperament, even in those far-off times; and although to-day the idea of it may call forth expressions of wonder, it was not, all things considered, so very surprising that it should have been so.

So the first of the converted witches perpetuated into the new order of things quite a goodly few of the old customs that hitherto had been associated with the practice of pagan witchcraft.

On the other hand, the converted witches who had espoused the new faith and then later on had broken their vows, returned to their old gods and to their old form of worship, but retained much of the new ritual that had been taught them. Thus the witches of the early centuries not only observed a

Sabbath, a Dedication, and a Sacrament, but they possessed a Baptistry ; and their meetings, or "covens" as they were called, only functioned when they consisted of thirteen : twelve witches and a chief, as though to burlesque the twelve disciples with their Master.

The combination or confusion of such ritual was of course a bad one. It did not work well. Indeed, it could not. A state of rivalry between the witches and the Christians came into being, each section striving to gain mastery over the other ; and while the Christians called upon Saints and Angels to aid them in their task, the witches co-opted all the Powers of Darkness from the nether world that they could think of. It has also been affirmed that the witches, as fanatical Dianists, endeavoured to outnumber the Christians by their own prolific progeny, while at the same time they cast spells over them, and poisoned their children. Such was the popular indictment.

Witchcraft, having its real inception in that period of fear, wonder, and sacrifice which is common to all primitives, passed through the long centuries in an ever-changing order of observance and behaviour, and, truth to tell, the change was not always for the better. The witchcraft of the third century and earlier, as shall be shown, was very different—possibly better, according to how one looks at it—from the witchcraft of the twelfth century ; and that of the thirteenth to the eighteenth changed successively with the centuries through which it passed.

Just to the extent that it was taught and believed from the third century onwards that the witches were " devil's servants," so it was also believed that witchcraft was " devil's work." Its adherents, to do their work the more effectively, swore allegiance to him, and to seal the compact it was necessary in accordance with the custom of the craft to renounce God. Whatever else they were, they were souls in revolt ; in fact, they were Anti-Christ, and that with a vengeance. Their feeling towards all authority was such that they could imagine nothing more revolutionary than to bring about an *inversion* of Christianity. One part of their ritual, that of chaunting the Lord's Prayer backwards, and another, centuries later, that of helping to bring into existence what has come to

be known as " The Wicked Bible," with the
" Thou shalt not commit adultery " of the
seventh commandment printed to read " Thou
shalt," show this very clearly.

That the performances of the witches in
England—with their Magic ; their Casting of
Spells ; Overlooking with the Evil Eye ;
their Sabbaths ; the Power of Divination ;
and the accredited exercise of what was called
Supernatural Power—were of grave concern
to the early Fathers, who were responsible
for public morality, is certain ; for we find
that Theodore, Archbishop of Canterbury, in
the seventh century forbade such practices
as incorporated the offering of " Sacrifices
to Devils," or " Eating in Heathen Temples,
including the celebrating of feasts in abominable places of the heathen, and of offering
and consuming food there " ; such practices
being part of the ritual of the witches. There
was also an edict issued by him forbidding
anyone " to dress in the skin of a wild animal,"
or " to go about as a stag or a bull," under a
penalty of three years' penance. This latter
edict most certainly referred to the animal
disguises which were so prominent both in
early Nature-worship and at the later " Sabbath of Witches "—a feast where it was

customary for the chief witch to play the part of devil dressed in the skin of a goat, stag, or bull, and wearing horns upon the head.

It may be inferred that such practices as the foregoing, which were forbidden by Theodore in the seventh century, had not abated in the eighth, and moreover, that they had become so general as to be known quite widely as " witchcraft," for we find Egbert, Archbishop of York, in this latter century forbidding the people to make " Offerings to Devils." The laws of the Northumbrian priests also made it known that " If anyone be found that shall henceforth practise any heathenships, *or in any wise love witchcraft*, he shall, if he be king's thane, pay X half-marks, one half to Christ and the other half to the king."

Two centuries later, a still greater effort seems to have been made to eradicate the witchcraft ritual, or at least to separate the ritual of the witches from the feasts of the Church, for the Ecclesiastical Canons enjoined every priest of the Church " zealously to promote Christianity and totally extinguish all heathenism, enchantments and other vain practices carried on by spells with Elders, trees

and stones; and also on *feast-days* to abstain
from heathen songs and devils' games."

By the twelfth century, as none of the
afore-mentioned edicts were successful in sup-
pressing the witches, stronger measures were
applied. Christianity had by then become
powerful enough to deal sternly with all
opponents, and there was issued the proclamation that " If witches or foul defiled
adulteresses be found anywhere within the
land, then let them be driven out from the
country, and the people cleansed; or *let
them totally perish* "; which injunction, for
centuries afterwards, was most rigorously
observed.

CHAPTER II

INITIATION AND CEREMONY

THE familiar term " witch " applied to either women or men, and " coven " was the word used to describe both their meetings and their meeting-place.

In the Middle Ages the word " covent " or " convent " was used for describing a *religious* assembly.[1] By slow stages the word " coven " came to be used to describe *any* gathering of twelve people with a leader—thirteen in all. So far as the witches were concerned, the word stood for a company of twelve witches, with their chief who impersonated the Devil.[2]

The witches' meeting-place was secret except to the members of the coven, and each

---

[1] Thus " Covent Garden," a well-known district in London, has evolved from " Convent-garden " : the garden of a Convent that once stood there.

[2] Pitcairn, in his *Criminal Trials of Scotland* (1362), says : " Ther wold sometymes meit a Coeven, and in ilk Coeven ther is threttein persones."

coven or meeting was presided over by someone whose real identity was known only to
the supreme chief of the craft. He was the
Master of the Ceremonies, quite unknown
to the rank and file except as a devil; and,
to aid him in his deception, he would arrive
and depart dressed in sombre brown or
black of a uniform pattern. To help him
further in his deceit he would wear a false
double-face, through which he was supposed
to speak [1]—like the old god Janus. At
other times he would wear a goat's face over
his own, and a mask or another false face
behind; sometimes this would be worn at
the back of the head, but more often than
not, very low down on the back, at the
bottom of the spine.

[1] The wondering mind asks whether the black "pope-
faces" worn by ragged urchins about the Fifth of November "in memory of Guy Fawkes" have nothing in particular to do with that Bolshevik, but have instead a
relationship—forgotten, may be—to the black Beelze-
bubs of the witches' covens?

In a Dorsetshire newspaper as late as the year 1911,
there was mention of an "ooser," or wooden mask, which
might very well be one of the old devil-faces; and,
strangely enough, it figured in a charge against a man
who had frightened girls by running after them when
he was "dressed in a bullock's skin and wearing an
ooser." Surely a survival of the bad old witchcraft days.

Besides the god Janus to whom we have just referred, there was the goddess Diana, both beloved of the early fraternity of witches. Whereas Janus was a god of fertility and patron saint of the cross-roads, having control over both the sun and moon, Diana, moon goddess, "Queen of the Night," was patron saint of both virginity and fertility. To her the cross-roads, where the witches often held their Feast of the Sabbath and other strange ordinances, were dedicated and sacred ; she possessed the further dreaded power of being able to send plagues and other awful things upon both man and beast.

One of the first and therefore one of the most valuable among mediæval writers to notice the Witches' Sabbath and its connection with the goddess Diana seems to have been Regino, Abbot of Prume, who at the end of the ninth century wrote of " wicked women who say they attend great meetings by night with Diana the goddess of the pagans to do her bidding."

Also identified with the goddess Diana was Hecâte, an earth-goddess, possessed of extensive power and honoured in turn by all the lesser gods. As a deity of the lower world she was a powerful divinity. She was supposed to send to those upon whom she deigned to pay her attention all kinds of demons and terrible phantoms by night. In addition, she is credited with having taught sorcery and witchcraft; to have dwelt where two roads crossed, on tombs, or near ground unhallowed by the spilling of human blood; to have wandered about with the souls of the dead in her possession; and to have had her presence made known by the piteous whining or howling of dogs.[1] Tradition has it that she was a hard and strict taskmaster, and that many a witch went about bearing visible signs of stripes inflicted upon their bodies because they had vexed her.

We should mention here, perhaps, the terrible witch goddess Erichtho, who was claimed to have wandered about tombs, from which she drew their ghosts. With funeral torches and with the ashes of the dead she worked her spells; her incantations were Stygian; by pressing her lips to

---

[1] Even to-day in many parts of the country the whining of a dog is heard with fear and a horror of something terrible happening. In the West and North of England it is looked upon as a sure sign of death to someone in the house outside which the dog makes his howl.

those of a dying man she sent messages to the under-world.

Every district seems to have had its coven, and local meetings were usually held once a week ; but the " Sabbath of Witches," held four times a year, and usually on a Thursday, for some strange reason, was the more important of the gatherings. The person or devil under whose superintendence it functioned was referred to as Beelzebub, Satan, Lucifer, or some other generally appropriate name. This presiding devil was, to the members of the coven, GOD ! On the knee they worshipped him with due acknowledgment as the giver of all things bad and indifferent. So strong indeed was the coven's belief in his power, and so much was he adored, that the witches even dedicated their children to his service, and, it has been averred, even offered them up to him in sacrifice.[1]

Every hamlet, it was declared, had its witch midwife who dedicated the babes to Satan as they were born. Thus children grew up " in the service," and it has been

[1] One of these fearful rites is indicated in a charge brought against Apollonius of Tyana when tried before Domitian (300 B.C.).

narrated how on one occasion a young girl innocently revealed to her unsuspecting father that she had the power to bewitch, and how in his horror he madly " informed " on his wife, who was charged, convicted, and burned.[1]

Just as the witches had their midwives, ever mindful of the craft, so had the Church theirs. The " recognised " midwives were licensed by the ecclesiastical authorities, and it was their duty, primarily, to see that all infants were baptised as quickly as possible after birth, before the witches had time or opportunity for working their evil spells over them. So important was the baptising of the infant considered, that if no priest was able to be present to perform the ceremony the midwife had authority to administer the Sacrament. These recognised midwives were not women, but *men*, and were in evidence until the seventeenth century.

Other officers holding subordinate positions in the coven were chosen by the witches themselves from their own particular coven; and here we might remark that as late as the seventeenth century it was declared by Cotton Mather, of Massachusetts—a Congregational minister, playing a most promi-

[1] *c.* 1430.

nent part in witch-hunting and witch-trials
—that " the witches' covens were governed
like Congregational Churches"! These subordinate officers were known as "minor
devils," and it was their duty to make note
of the local attendances, to initiate new converts, to set the pace in the witches' dance,
and to make themselves generally useful in
other ways.

Once in every seven years there would
be what was called a " Great Sabbath," at
which all the covens of a wide district would
congregate, and tradition has it that on that
occasion the Chief Witch or "Devil" himself was sacrificed. This particular sacrifice may of course have been nothing more
or less than deception, but it must be remembered that every tradition enshrines
some element of truth.

The actual initiation into the mysteries of
witchcraft must have been an exciting experience. The aspirant to membership, after
being duly recommended, would have to be
introduced ; and the manner of introduction
would be kept secret until the actual event.
Before the assembled coven there would be a
renouncement on the part of the candidate
of any former faith to which there had been

an adherence, and then the presiding Master of the Ceremonies or Chief Devil would proceed with the service as follows :

Placing one hand on the crown of the head of the candidate and the other on the sole of the foot, he would declare that from now henceforward all that was betwixt and between his two hands—body and soul—were at the Devil's service. Pitcairn, in his *Criminal Trials*, mentions how at a Dalkeith witch-trial a reputed witch named Janet Watson confessed that when she was initiated into the craft, the presiding devil laid his hand on her head saying "all" that was under it was his "from now onward"!

After the reception the candidate would be baptised with a new name, such as "Thief of Heaven" or some other horrid appellation, by which "it" would be afterwards known.

There is a greater significance about this change of name than is apparent at first sight, for it was one of the essentials to complete witchcraft. The witches' masters were crafty tutors and, moreover, psychologists of no mean order. They knew that so long as there was a remembrance on the part of their converts as to who they were or what they had been, there would be too keen a sense of decorum for them to prove good witches. With change of name there came a change in the atmosphere of association; and a change of behaviour, shaped with an utter disregard for what had been restraining social influences, is not far off. Human nature is a strange quantity, and usually lives up to what is expected of it; so the neophytes were given a new name—" Devil's Whelp," or something of the sort—and every action henceforth would be prompted by a desire to be worthy of it.

Besides, there was another object at the back of the idea, and probably a more important one than that just referred to. It was thought that if a person was unfortunate enough to be assailed by evil spirits, that same person could dodge them by a change of name. Thus if, say, someone by the name of Tompkins suffered grievously on account of, as it was thought, the amount of attention given to him by the powers of darkness, and he changed his name to Smith, Jones, Brown, or Robinson, the evil spirits would lose track of him, as they would be on the lookout for Tompkins, who had, according to the old line of argument, become absolutely nonexistent by jettisoning his name overboard.

The reader will remember the account in the New Testament of the Gadarene hypochondriac possessed of devils. When Jesus said to him, " What is thy name ? " he replied, "My name is Legion, for we are many." Thus it may be inferred that the man believed he had no name—it had been lost in the hideous tyranny of that multitude of demons under whose influence his own personality had been destroyed. Also, if the reader will pardon the intrusion, there is a further explanation and a continuity of the idea in the authorised version of the New Testament, where in St. Mark's Gospel we learn that as Jesus went with his disciples to the sea of Galilee unclean spirits fell down before him; that he ordained twelve, having power to cast out devils: Simon he surnamed Peter, meaning a rock; and James and John he surnamed Boanerges, which means " the Sons of Thunder "—in the very names of which there is inspiration.

So, as many of the witches were " throwbacks " from the Christians who believed that they were safeguarded from evil by good spirits, they would change their names so that they might escape the good spirits' watchfulness, for they had become the workers

of darkness. They did not want to be good.
Besides, the new name " Thief of Heaven "
suggested the kind of work that was expected
of them.

When the new name had been given, the
witch would be admonished in a most fearful manner to keep the witch-commandment,
which was, in brief, to do all the harm
possible ; but to tell no secrets.

If there was a betrayal of confidences on
the part of members, woe betide them, for
punishment was given—actually—with a rod
of iron. So close was the order and so
perfect was the witch-preservation system,
that if once there was the merest suspicion
of betrayal of confidence, the punishment
would be inflicted, and it would be made to
extend even to one of death upon further
guilt. Even confinement in prison, following
a charge of witchcraft before the justices,
was not sufficient protection against the long
arm or the power of the coven's chief if confessions were made at the trial of a witch
undergoing examination. In one case of an
oncoming witch-trial, when a confession or
a blurting out of secrets on the part of one
of the witches was feared, the emissaries of
the chief of the coven actually got by stealth

into the prison where the wretched witch was incarcerated, and hanged him before he had the chance of committing the anticipated indiscretion—believing, of course, that the dead can tell no tales!

As a favourite accomplishment of the witch, and one that she was considered to be most proficient in, was that of poisoning, the poison would be handed round to the witches by the chief of the coven as they sat or knelt in a circle. Their usual posture for receiving it was to squat on the ground with knees drawn up to chin and hands clasped before them, their bodies rocking backward and forward to the accompaniment of some wretched dirge or chant composed of a string of apparently meaningless jargon, such as "Shurius, Turius, Tirus," and so on; [1] still kneeling and with their hair tumbling loose over their shoulders, their skinny hands held

[1] In our own time the children of the village have a jargon which they go through in a very painstaking manner when playing at what is styled "touch." Has it, one wonders, a relationship with the old spells? Phonetically it is as follows:

Eener, deener, dyner, dust,
Cattell-err-weeler, wyler, wust,
Twiddle-um, Twoddle-um, Twenty-one,
Spit, spot, must be done—Out goes she.

aloft, they would receive the potion, handed to them with a curse upon it. So skilful were they in their use of it, and so awful was the fear of it, that Henry VIII fitted the punishment to the crime of poisoning by a statute authorising that poisoners should, upon conviction, be BOILED !

The initiation ceremony usually ended by the whole gathering being adjured to salute their chief in the usual manner, which was, in brief, by kissing him on the false face that he wore at the bottom of his back. In acknowledgment of such gallantry the convert would receive " a witches' mark " : a kind of blood-blister or " blew spot " on the left side of the body, under the arm, or on the shoulder. It was caused by a nipping of the flesh with a tweezer-like instrument, and at this mark or teat the witch's " familiar " imp or demon would later on come and take nourishment— so it was supposed, and verily believed.

When the foregoing infernal performance was really concluded, the witches believed themselves to turn into cats, hares, rooks, or bats, and depart, riding on broomsticks or on goats, pigs, or dogs, to great distances.

As showing how to some extent the witches'

performances were a burlesque upon those of
the Christian, and not devoid of a tinge
of fear, it is interesting to note that before
the flight the witches were warned not to
mention the name of " Jesus " when fly-
ing, or they would fall to the ground. In
nearly all the " mysteries " being played by
the clericals of those early years—mention
of which is made a few pages farther on—and
in which devils appeared, the mere whisper
of the sacred name was enough to make them
disappear instantly. This on the part of the
clericals was to demonstrate to the people
that good was more powerful than evil. It
is perhaps remarkable that the witches, having
once accepted the belief, could not rid themselves of it.

The actual flight of the witch was of course
imaginative, and the result of, probably,
among other things, auto-suggestion ; or it
may have been due to the effects of " witches'
ointment," a concoction composed of herbs
and obnoxious ingredients, and said to include
the brains of unbaptised infants—grave-
robbed.[1] More than likely it gave off some

[1] The habit of robbing graves was not only put to the
credit of the witches, for in old records it is clear that
fairies did not escape the charge of doing so. In some

hypnotic, sleep-inducing, mind-muddling odour when sufficient of it was smeared on the naked bodies of the witches attending the coven.[1]

Reginald Scot, in his *Discoverie of Witch-craft* (1584), gives the following concoction of ointment as being used for the " transportation " of witches from one place to another :

" The fat of young children, and seeth it with water in a brazen vessell, reserving the thickest of that which remaineth boiled at the bottom which they lay up and keep until occasion serveth to use it. They put hereunto Eleoselinum Aconitum, belladonna, soote and Solanum Somniferum. They mix all these together, and then they rub all parts of their bodies exceedingly till they look red and be very hot, so as the pores may be opened and their flesh soluble and loose. They join herewithal either fat or

parts of Scotland, and perhaps in England also, it is a belief that even living infants can be *stolen or changed* by the fairies, and to prevent such a calamity the infants are closely watched until the christening has taken place. No harm can come to them then from the fairies. It is claimed by some writers that the words " fairy " and " witch " are synonymous.

[1] This may have been instituted by the witches as a ridiculous imitation of Christian immersions and anointings.

oil that the force of the ointment may pierce inwards and so be more effectual. By this means on a moonlight night they seem to be carried in the air to feastings, singings, dancing, kissings, embracings and other acts." These Sabbath ceremonies were in reality a form of devil worship not unlike those that have formed part of the belief of most primitive peoples and races. As, for instance, in Hindu superstition the witches by means of mystic spells fly naked to their meeting place, where they dance the night away, etc.

Belladonna probably being the chief ingredient of the ointment, it would certainly have the effect of producing vascular excitement, with hallucinations. Other roots and plants such as mandrake and poppy, foxglove, and so on, all found a usefulness in the witches' pharmacopœia. Bacon said of the mandrake that it was "a root whereof witches made an ugly image, giving it the form of a face on the top of the root." A wine made from the root had the effect of sending those that drank of it into deep sleep, from which on awaking all manner of things would be imagined. It has been called "the insane root which takes the reason prisoner."

Upon recovering from its effects, a person

would be wild and fearful, and often shrieking would accompany the coming to.   Hence
the saying, " shrieking like mandrakes."

" And shrieks like mandrakes torn out of the earth,
That living mortals hearing them run mad."
(*Romeo and Juliet.*)

In gathering or uprooting the root certain
rites and ceremonies had to be performed,
or it would not do its work well.   An ancient
writer, Josephus, says :

" To gather ye mandragora, go forthe at dead of
nyght and take a dogge or other animal and tye hym
wyth a corde unto ye plante.   Loose ye earth round
about ye roote, then leave hym, for in his struggles to
free hymself he will teare up ye roote whych by its
dreadfull cryes wyll kyll ye animal."

Its " dreadfull cryes " would be drowned
by someone standing by blowing a horn.
It was also used under the name of
" morion " or " death wine " to render insensible those about to suffer torture.   Hence
under Roman rule, Jewish women would administer it to those who were being crucified.
It would allay suffering and wrap the soul in
night.   It was on account of the crucified
often recovering after they had been removed
from the cross, as dead, that the Roman
soldiers were ordered to mutilate the bodies

before they were handed over to their friends for burial.

Its use for purposes of enchantment were also widely recognised. To the Babylonians and the Egyptians it was a charm against sterility, and was known to them as " the phallus of the field "; and to judge from the story connected with an episode in the life of Rachel (Genesis xxx.), the ancient Hebrews also believed it to possess a special virtue in this respect.

The psycho-analytical significance attached to the belief of the witches, that they went riding through the air, as just mentioned, may be found perhaps in the idea and belief that from time immemorial the goat, the pig, the many-teated sow, the dog, and especially the cat, have been supposed to be possessed of some magic power of protection or charm for fecundity, and it was probably for that reason the witches adopted one or other of them as a kind of mascot; *cf.* the idea that the witches by their prolific progeny would help them to smother the Christians.

Of all living things connected with super-stitious belief in general, and with witches in particular, the cat holds a by no means unimportant place.   In early Egyptian days it was deified and worshipped, sacrifices were offered and temples were dedicated to it.   Along with Diana, it was revered as an emblem of the moon, and when it died the people in many a household would show their sorrow by shaving their eyebrows.   And speaking of eyebrows reminds us of how the meeting of the eyebrows above the bridge of the nose on the physiognomy of any one person was considered in many parts of the world until a hundred or so years ago to be a sure sign that the owner of the eyebrows would die either a witch or a vampire.   Not only was the meeting of the eyebrows taken for the sign and prognostication ; but a dropping eyelid, a squint, or any other malformation of the eye or eyelids, was considered an un-questionable proof of the possession of the witch-power of " overlooking," or of the casting of spells.   In the famous trial of the Lancashire witches it was remarkable that the most notorious characters, according to tradition, all possessed a definite and deplor-ably comical squint.   In nearly all the old pictures of witches riding to their rendezvous on birchbrooms or sows, they are portrayed with what are commonly referred to as "funny eyes," and accompanied into the bargain by a knowing-looking black cat.

Among other magic powers attributed to witches was that of turning *themselves* into cats—real cats! In this manner the cat eventually became the symbol of the witch, and by another quick-change the representation of the Devil. To this day some people affirm the same metamorphosis takes place.

In the trial of Bartie Paterson, in 1607, it was given as evidence that the accused *was a witch* because she had disguised herself *as a cat*, and had, with other cats—that is, witches—given a serenade on a certain and particular night in the backyard of one of the witnesses appearing at the trial. The evidence was believed, and Bartie was hanged. Surely so accomplished a contortionist was not deserving of being overtaken by such a catastrophe.

The cat also played an important part among the witches' "familiars," for in many a trial it was declared that "the witch's familiar in the shape of a little dun cat as smooth as a mole" used to lay on the witch's right breast until the witch went into a kind of stupor.

The throwing of a cat into water was

believed to be a means of raising a storm
at sea for the sinking of ships and the drowning of men and women over whom a spell
had been cast. This charge figured in at
least one very important trial, particulars
of which are given later on. On another
occasion some reputed witches were caught
actually throwing a cat into the sea so that
King James might lose his life as he was
journeying from Scotland to Denmark.

This latter, occupying as it does so interesting a niche in the annals of witchcraft, is
well deserving here of a little attention, and
especially as Christiania, the capital of Norway, so closely associated with the event, has
just been brought prominently to our notice
on account of its name being changed to that
of Oslo. It was at Oslo, in the year 1589,
that King James VI of Scotland, afterwards
James I of England (who figures so prominently in the story of the witches), married
the Dano-Norwegian princess, Anne, daughter
of Frederick II. The events leading up to
James's notoriety with regard to witch-trials
are as follows :

After negotiations concerning the dowry
had been satisfactorily settled, and James's
Lord Stewart's arrangements for the wedding

had been agreed to by the Queen Dowager,
Sophia—King Frederick having died in the
meantime—Copenhagen, at which place the
princess resided, began to get busy and to
show signs that something untoward was
happening. The excitement reached its
climax when, on September 1st, 1589, a fleet
of twelve vessels, with the princess on board
the grander of them, set sail from Copenhagen
for Scotland.

All would have gone well with it had not
the witches of Norway and the witches of
Scotland thought fit to object to the whole
proceedings. Consequently, when the fleet
sailed it soon got into difficulties. It was
encompassed by tremendous seas and blown
about by hurricanes of the worst description ;
so much so, indeed, that to make headway
was impossible. Therefore, after fifty-two
days of battling with the elements, it had
perforce to return to Oslo. James, on his
part, was fretting his soul away in Scotland
for the best part of those fifty-two days ;
then when the suspense of waiting could
be endured no longer, he set sail himself for
Norway, and arrived at Oslo actually before
the return of the princess. The meeting,
according to the chroniclers, was ludicrous.

The wedding, however, took place a few days later, and the royal pair left Oslo for Scotland a month afterwards.

Now for the sequel. The witches—confound them!—had dared to interfere with a king's intentions : surely they should be made to pay the penalty. So there was a round-up of witches at Oslo, a number of them being subsequently burned ; then the round-up was transferred to Scotland in general and to Berwick in particular, where there was arrested among other alleged witches a man named Johanne Feane. This man was put on trial. The indictment, or rather one of the twenty indictments, against him was that with others he had entered into a compact with Satan to wreck the king's ship on its way to Oslo. Another count was, that while the king was on his journey, Feane, with a whole company of other witches, did by arrangement with Satan meet on the high seas, and did there throw an enchanted cat into the water with the intention of drowning the king in a terrific storm of wind that was caused thereby : and also, that upon the king's return to Scotland he, with other witches, did get Satan to promise the witches to create such a mist as would wreck the king's

ship on the English coast. (The reason why
the king did not get drowned in the storm
that raged and the mist that rose was that
James, being a man of God, would allow
none of these perils, charms, and devilries
to prevail against him.)

Another charge brought against Feane was
that on an occasion specified he did go to
North Berwick Church, and with a corpse-
candle did spring the lock so that the door
opened to his magic, and that when he got
inside he did consort with Satan and a number
of witches and did take part in an infernal
service where Satan himself (described as a
little black man with a single black beard
like a goat's, a rabbit-nose, and a long tail,
and dressed in a brownish gown) did enter
the pulpit and from a big black book which
he carried about with him did preach unto
them, saying, " Fear not, though I am grim,
I have many servants who shall not want
so long as they spare not to do evil. . . .
Be blithe : eat, drink, and take ease. . . .
You shall be raised up gloriously when you
fly " (and much more burlesque of a similar
nature). Would Johanne Feane confess to
these charges ? No ! Not if he could help
it, for he was a man of some refinement, even

in those days of sparse learning; and withal, was he not the schoolmaster of Salpans, with a reputation to keep up? and was it not a fact that the charge of witchcraft would never have been brought against him at all had not a whitewasher, of whose work he had occasion to complain, thought it an excellent manner of revenge? But that availed him nothing. A charge had only to be made and the rest was easy. There were then, as there are to-day, ever so many more perjurers than the world has need for.

If he will not confess his guilt willingly, then he must be tortured until he does; so, two pins, each about three inches in length, are driven through the tongue, to their heads. Here his courage fails him, as well it might, and he makes confession; but so soon as the pins are withdrawn he recants. Then other perjurers come forward and declare that they had seen him chasing cats over hedges, and that when they had asked him why he was doing it he had replied that he "wanted them for Satan," and that "Satan wanted as many as he could catch, for to throw them into the sea that the king might be drowned." Other witnesses came forward to give evidence of his casting of horoscopes, but enough had already been said to flame the sky red o'er Edinburgh's Castle Hill. Confessions, and further confessions, were then demanded. They were not forthcoming. So he was put to the torture of the crusher (the boot), and on fainting from the agony of it, they said the Devil had made him stubbornly insensible to pain, or he would have cried out. Upon "coming to" his courage fails him, and he confesses, but says the most ridiculous and absurd things possible ; not caring much what is to happen, for he has made his peace with God. This, however, somewhat pleases those before whom he is arraigned, and he is taken to his cell for further examination on the morrow, but when in his cell his conscience calls him " coward " for confessing, so once more he plays the man and recants. Next day, on account of his quietness during the night, they said the Devil had visited him. He denies the truth of their statement. So they reply to the effect that they will search for the mark the Devil has left behind him, upon which they tear off with pincers every finger-nail—to find the mark ; and perpetrate other tortures too horrible to mention. But there are no more confessions. He prefers rather to die bravely. So " on a Saterdaie in the end of Januarie 1591" he is first strangled and then "burned in the Castle Hill of Edinbrough"—and, as an old chronicler has recorded, "It did give the king a great and pleasurable satisfaction of mind."

In this account of the trial of Feane, mention has been made of "witches' candles." What these were in reality it is difficult to say, but according to tradition they were made by witches in the moonlight, and were composed of hair from a hanged man, fat from the witches' cauldron into which had been thrown all and more of the fearful things already mentioned in preceding pages of this book, together with the finger of a murderer, grave-robbed. Upon one of these candles being held to a lock the spring would fly back as if by magic and the most heavily bolted and barred door would open.

Of course it is all very horrible; but say— is it, after allowing for traditional exaggeration, so very much worse than some other things then recognised as scientific? For instance, the following is not a witches' concoction for the working of spells, but extracts from the *London Pharmacopœia* of 1618. The ingredients mentioned here are all

recommended to be used in medical prescriptions for the curing of one thing or another :
" Blood, Fat, Bile, Bones, Claws, Teeth, Hoofs, Horns, Eggs of Insects, Scorpions, Feathers, Hair, Isinglass, Placenta, Bone Marrow, Cocks-comb, Cuttle-fish, Spider-webb, Cast-off-snakes-Skin, Saliva from a Fasting Man, and Bones from the Skull of a Criminal."

All things considered, there can be no doubt but that the witches' meetings, notwithstanding their grotesque character, became extremely popular, and that their ritual or form of ceremony *was* the sort of thing that *did* really appeal to numberless people. And after all, it was not perhaps so very different from other strange religious orders that were in existence, if not in England, in other parts of the world where the inhabitants were certainly not less enlightened.

Considering the manner in which the witches' devotions or services had perforce to be conducted in secrecy and by stealth, the wonder is that they throve at all ; unless it be by reason of the perversity of human nature finding delight in doing the things it should not.

The witches' order of service for the most part was based on, or inspired by, their knowledge of the amount of adoration given to religious relics placed in Christian shrines, and the witches being of a revolutionary character, yet not without a sense of humour, burlesqued, though in a vulgar fashion, every formality connected therewith. Their covens, as has been stated, were in imitation of the Twelve Disciples ; they boasted of a dedication, a sacrament, and a Sabbath. True discipleship meant complete surrender of self to their chief who was as God; and even the three faces of their Beelzebub was an imitation of an early idea of the Trinity, depicted in very old pictures as a person with three heads on one pair of shoulders. The kissing of Beelzebub as a token of allegiance on the lower face worn by him, was probably a burlesque on those of a different creed who at the time of the origin of the custom were said to enjoy a sense of holiness by kissing a buttock-bone of one of the saints then being carried about the country by a Jesuit priest—much in the same manner as some folk to this day devoutly kiss a stone imitation of Peter's big-toe.

The enticing character of the witches' meetings were well known to the clergy of the day as being in competitive opposition to their own religious cause, and it was not to be encouraged. The witches, for their part, were out to catch converts; so was the Church. Each strove to get the better of the other. Of course the Church won; that was a foregone conclusion; but what arts did she not have to employ in the winning! As though the usual order of service was not attractive enough, it had to be added to. Other attractions had to be thought out, and sure enough, as though from Heaven, the very thing they were looking for was at hand. Indeed, it was at their doors, and all that had to be done was to acquire and equip it according to their own particular requirements. What this was and how it came to be made use of to the detriment of the witches, is as follows :—

From the eighth century onwards trade was principally carried on by means of fairs, which lasted several days. The merchants of the early Dick Whittington type who frequented these fairs in numerous caravans and companies employed every art to draw the people round. They were therefore accompanied by jugglers, minstrels, and

buffoons who exerted all the skill they possessed and reserved for the occasion. As but
few large towns were then in existence, no
fixed popular amusement existed, and as
society functions were unknown the fair-time
was the season for entertainment. In proportion as these shows were attended and
encouraged they were from time to time set
off with new decorations and improvements ;
and the art of buffoonery becoming more
attractive, they acquired a position of real
importance in the lives of the people. By
degrees the clergy observing that the enter-
tainments of music, dancing, and mimicry
exhibited at the fairs made the people more
frivolous and less religiously inclined, and
thinking besides that here was a good opportunity for the acquisition of something that
appealed to them in their new efforts of
diverting the wicked from the witches' covens,
not only proscribed the shows but excommunicated the performers and turned actors
themselves. Henceforth, instead of profane
mummeries they presented stage plays, based
upon religious legends, the lives of the saints,
or Bible mysteries : so called because they
enacted such narratives as those of the
Creation and the Nativity.

The first trace of these representations in England seems to have been about the year 1110, when, as is recorded by Matthew Paris, a learned Norman, master of the school of the Abbey of Dunstable, composed a play which was acted by the scholars who, for the said performance, borrowed copes from the sacrist of the Abbey of St. Albans to dress themselves in.

But that these mystery plays became in their turn most popular there can be no doubt, for Dugdale in his *History of Warwickshire* relates how before the suppression of the monasteries the city was very famous for them. They were played upon Corpus Christi Day, which had come to take the place of one of their ancient fair-days, founded in all probability by the pagans, and which brought people, even in those days of difficult travelling, from far-off parts. These pageants were acted with mighty state and reverence, and the celebrity of the performances may be inferred from the rank of the audiences, for in 1483 Richard III especially visited Coventry to see them, and a few years later Henry VII and his queen honoured them with their august presence.

These plays were given either out of doors

on meadowland surrounded by rising ground,
or in churches, barns, or other suitable build-
ings. Ordinarily the stage on which they
were given consisted of three platforms one
above the other. The uppermost platform
represented heaven, and on it sat whoever
was chosen to personate God, surrounded by
winged angels ; on the second, the glorified
saints; and on the lowest, ordinary human
men. On one side of the lowest platform was
a dark pitchy cavern sort of place, from
whence issued smoke of a distinctly bad
quality. From this yawning cave every now
and again the audience would be treated
with hideous yells and distracting noises in
imitation of the howlings and cries of wretched
souls tormented beyond description by re-
lentless demons. The one bit of sad humour
about the whole entertainment was, that at
frequent intervals the devils themselves would
ascend, to the immense delight of the audience,
and preach little homilies on correct living.

One of the most frequently acted and therefore popular performances was that known
as " The Ceremony of the Boy Bishop." It
was played in almost every parish in England
from the twelfth century until suppressed by
Henry VIII, and in more than one particular

is not so very much unlike what would certainly have been described as witchcraft if practised by any others than the clericals. The story on which the performance is based is as follows : A gentleman sending his two sons to a distant town for education ordered them to wait on St. Nicholas, Bishop of Myra in the fourth century, that he might bestow upon them his benediction. On arriving at their destination with their baggage they took up their lodging at an inn, intending, as it was then late in the day, to defer their visit till the morrow ; but in the meantime the rascally innkeeper, to secure their belongings for himself, killed the youths, cut them into pieces, salted them in a brine-tub, and intended to sell them on the morrow as pickled pork. St. Nicholas being favoured with a sight of these proceedings in a vision, went to the inn, and reproached the cruel landlord for his crime, who, immediately confessing it, entreated the saint to pray to Heaven for his pardon. The Bishop, moved by his confession and contrition, besought forgiveness for him, and supplicated restoration of life to those that had been killed. He had scarcely finished when, hey presto! the pieces reunited, and the animated youths threw themselves from the brine-tub at the Bishop's feet. He raised them up and exhorted them to return thanks, not to him, but to God. He then gave them good advice for their future guidance in life, bestowed his deferred blessing on them, and sent them with great joy to continue their studies.

Here, indeed, a miracle had been performed which was far and away more striking to the imagination than anything the witches were able to boast of; its memory was worth perpetuating. St. Nicholas became the patron saint of scholars and choir-boys, and simultaneously there came into existence that feast or performance which was afterwards known far and wide as " The Ceremony of the Boy Bishop."

The ceremony consisted of the boys of the choir meeting in solemn conclave and electing from themselves one who for a stated period would assume and maintain the state and authority of bishop, for which purpose he would be habited in rich episcopal robes, wear a mitre on his head, and carry a crosier in his hand. The other boys of the choir, assuming the character and dress of priests, yielded him canonical obedience, taking possession of the church and performing all the ceremonies except Mass. The Boy Bishop's term of authority would last from the 6th of December until the 28th of the same month, which was kept as Innocents' Day, in commemoration of Herod's murder of the children. As we have said, the ceremony became very popular, and Brand in his *Antiquities* mentions how " it became a custom to whip up the children upon Innocents day morning that the memorie of Herods murther might stick the closer ; in moderate proportion," he adds, " this whipping up of the children did act over again the cruelty in kind."

On the authority of an old ritual belonging to the Abbey of Oseney it would appear that at the church of Oseney " they were wont to bring out upon that day the foot of a child prepared after their fashion, and put upon with red and black colours, as to signify the dismal part of the day. They put this up in a chest in the vestry, ready to be produced at the time, and to be solemnly carried about the church as a relic to be adored by the people."

An amusing fact concerning the foregoing is that although there are only two youths in the story, the contemporary pictures of the miracle show *three* youths coming out of the brine-tub. Evidently the story was thought good enough to be made the most of. Incidentally, one wonders whether St. Nicholas's association with the brine-tub has any connection with his being the patron saint of the sailors.

On the Continent such ceremonies were even more surprising, so much so, in fact, that the witches' performances were dull and insignificant by comparison; such were the times, however, that there was applause for the clericals, and burnings for the witches, although the doings of the one were just as silly as the doings of the other. Take, for instance, another description of a mystery play, this time the "Creation," the accuracy of which is vouched for by Hone in his work, *Mystery Plays and Ecclesiastical Shows*.

Let us imagine that we are attending one of these old plays : The improvised theatre where the mystery is to be performed is a barn with one side or end of it taken away completely, thus leaving what is an ideal stage for the purpose. The inside is in darkness, as is observed when the great tapestry curtains are drawn aside. A sleepy-looking Capuchin comes to the front. He wears a large, full-bottomed wig and a long beard. Over his rusty dress is a brocade morning-gown, the lining of blue silk being occasionally visible on account of the pride the wearer takes in the showing of it ; his slippers of blue silk being eyed and shown with equal satisfaction. He is personating the Creator. He makes his way through the tapestry, groping about ; and purposely runs his head against a post, upon which he exclaims, " Let there be light ! " His request is complied with by someone drawing aside more curtains, so that from the interior a dim glimmer from a few small lamps is observable. The creation of the sea is represented by the pouring of water along the stage, and the making of dry land by the throwing of mould. Angels are personated by girls and young priests habited in dresses hired from a masquerade shop, to which the wings of geese are clumsily attached at the shoulders. These angels then become active in assisting the character in the dressing-gown to produce the stars, moon, and sun from a pile of miscellaneous articles got together for the occasion. To represent winged fowl, a number of cocks and hens of the domestic variety are fluttering about, and for other living creatures some cows, goats, a well-shod horse, and two pigs with rings already in their noses are driven across the stage.

Then Adam appears, a great clumsy fellow in a full wig, and being but scantily clad looks amusingly grotesque. He stalks about wonderingly and is followed by a large ugly mastiff wearing a brass collar with spikes on it. Presently, when he reclines on the stage preparatory to the production of Eve, the dog lays down beside him, which obedience on the part of the dog occasions some embarassment on account of " the creator " not being able to proceed with the idea he has in mind. However, the angels behind the wooden clouds eventually whistle the dog off and all goes well again.

The performance proceeds by the extraction of a rib from the dog's master, which, on being brought forward and shown to the audience, is carried back again to be changed into Eve, who in order to be seen as though rising out of Adam's side is dragged up from the side of him that is farthest away from the audience, through an ill-concealed and equally ill-contrived trap-door. Then the dog comes back, having broken away from those that would hold him in captivity, and lays down once more by the side of Adam who is still sleeping and snoring loudly to show that there is no fraud being played. As Eve is being lifted over Adam the dog unfortunately gets trod upon, with the result that it makes a snap at the M.C., who, being frightened, drops Eve plomp on Adam's chest. As this is the fault of the dog, it gets a hearty kick and so walks off sulkily, but returns after a few minutes with the rib in his mouth. *He* had discovered it, and it more resembled a bullock's rib than the rib of a man.

Eve's part is being personated by a young priest of effeminate appearance but awkward in form, with long locks composed of something like strands of rope which hang stiffly down the back and are brought round to fasten in a knot in front below the waist. Then the pair are driven out of paradise, and this is entrusted to a priest wearing wings, and with a fiery-looking imitation sword held aloft, which a moment later, on account of its having accidentally hit Adam on the head, is broken by that worthy gentleman into many fragments; an act which obviously chagrins the priest exceedingly, for he takes from under his habit the knotted

Capuchin rope he habitually wears, and applies it unmercifully to Adam's back. This forming as it did the grand finale, the curtains are drawn together, the play is ended, and everyone seems to be of the opinion that they feel all the better for having witnessed " a mysterie " which has been especially prepared for their enlightenment and edification.

In England, the most important mystery plays written and acted were the Coventry Mysteries of the fourteenth century, and when they were given before the public the parts of Adam and Eve were played in a state of nudity. In the second Pageant of Coventry manuscript in the British Museum it is indicated that when Eve is tempted by the serpent and induces Adam to taste of the fruit, he immediately perceives what until then he had been ignorant of, and says to her :

> Se us nakyd be for & be hynde,
>
> .   .   .   .   .
>
> Woman, lay this leaff on thee,
> And with this leaff I shall hyde me.

Warton observes that this extraordinary spectacle was beheld by a numerous company of both sexes with great composure.

The actors said they had the authority of Scripture for such a representation, and they gave things just as they found them in the third chapter of Genesis ; and if it had not been intended to have been so, it would not have been written.

When it is considered that one of the most severe indictments against the witches was that nudity entered into the ceremony of their Sabbath, it shows how akin in some respects the behaviour of each sect was to that of the other. Really, it would seem from such performances that the witches' burlesque of the Christians was one thing and that the clericals' burlesque, though equally reprehensible, was another.

Taking into consideration that the punishment of the witches was one of burning, it would seem that the burlesque of God by the clericals was then considered to be the lesser of the two evils. However, without drawing further comparisons, we will return to our main theme of witchcraft, from which we have been unwittingly side-tracked by the lure of the subject touched upon.

CHAPTER III

SPELLS, THE EVIL EYE, AND POSSESSION

Round about the cauldron go,
In the poison'd entrails throw.
Toad, that under cold stone
Days and nights has thirty-one
Swelter'd venom sleeping got,
Boil thou first i' the charmed pot.
       Double, double toil and trouble :
       Fire burn, and cauldron bubble.
Fillet of a fenny snake,
In the cauldron boil and bake ;
Eye of newt and toe of frog,
Wool of bat and tongue of dog,
Adder's fork and blind-worm's sting,
Lizard's leg and howlet's wing,
For a charm of powerful trouble,
Like a hell-broth boil and bubble.
       Double, double toil and trouble :
       Fire burn, and cauldron bubble.
Scale of dragon, tooth of wolf ;
Witches' mummy ; maw and gulf
Of the ravin'd salt-sea shark ;
Root of hemlock digg'd i' the dark,
Liver of blaspheming Jew ;
Gall of goat and slips of yew
Sliver'd in the moon's eclipse ;
Nose of Turk and Tartar's lips ;

Finger of birth-strangled babe
Ditch-deliver'd by a drab,
Make the gruel thick and slab ;
Add thereto a tiger's chauldron,
For the ingredients of our cauldron.
      Double, double toil and trouble :
      Fire burn, and cauldron bubble.
Cool it with a baboon's blood,
Then the charm is firm and good.

THIS interesting description of the witch and her poison potion is given, as the reader will remember, by Shakespeare, in the tragedy of *Macbeth*. The scene is a cavern on a blasted heath, in the middle of which is a boiling cauldron round about which three witches dance to the accompaniment of thunder, with lightning thrown in to give it scenic effect.

Just as the bubbling cauldron with its awful ingredients was essential to perfect witchcraft, so also were a number of small images made of lead or wax. These models were supposed to represent just those people upon whom the witches intended to work their spells, and they figured conspicuously in some famous witch-trials. These models were usually crude, but sometimes deftly fashioned; they were about the size of a thumb, and had scratched upon each the necessary name. Being of soft substance, lead or wax, they would melt if held before a fire or over a taper with suitable incantation, and as they became distorted or wasted away by the heat, so it was thought that the actual body of which they were the symbol would become distorted and wasted. If the victim was to suffer, say, a heart attack, the model would be pricked in the heart region, and so on.[1]

Here again, as in other instances, the origin of the belief in the witches' ability to injure, to have power over, or to cause suffering by the possession of a model representing whoever was to be afflicted, is to be found among the earliest of human beliefs. In the rude figures cut in stone by Palæolithic man, there are many representations of animals and wild beasts, and it may be conjectured that those primitive people carved the images of animals because they believed that being in possession of the image of such and such an animal gave them some peculiar power over the animal itself. *They did not carve or paint for the sake of art*. The animals they carved or painted in the caves were those they needed

[1] Plato speaks with reprobation of venal sorcerers who hired themselves out to those desirous of destroying with magic arts, incantations, and wax figures.

either for food or clothing, and were desirous of gaining mastery over. In a similar manner the witches believed they gained a mastery over their victims by being in possession of their effigy.[1]

Another manner of casting a spell was to take some earth from a newly-dug grave, then to rob a corpse of a rib-bone, burn it to ashes, and to mix the ingredients with black spider and the sap of elder.[2] Moulded into the shape of a frog or toad to represent the person to be spell-bound it would have pins or thorns stuck into it ; the victim would then come under the spell and the spell was supposed to kill the victim by the ninth day. If it did not, then poison would be requisitioned and there would be no more pinpricks or sleepless nights.

In a seventeenth-century treatise on witch-

[1] In our day we have the idea expressed on " Bonfire Night," or the burning in public of a newspaper with unpalatable ideas and whose proprietors are ungetatable.

[2] It is strange how among trees the elder thrives on a bad reputation. There are some folks who never refer to it except as " the stinking elder," and there are others who believe it to have been " the cursed tree " from which the cross was made upon which Christ was crucified, and also that it was the tree upon which Judas hanged himself. (*Vide* Shakespeare's *Love's Labour's Lost* and *Cymbeline*.)

craft this is described as follows : " Witches do torment mankind by making images of clay or wax, and when the witches prick or punce these images, the person whom these images represent do find extreme torment which doth not proceed from any influence these images have upon the body tormented, *but the devil doth by natural means* raise these torments in the person tormented, at the very same time that the witches do prick or punce or hold to the fire these images of clay or wax."

So acceptable to many minds have similar beliefs to this been for ages and ages that there should be little wonder concerning its wizardry.   For instance : in the reign of Romanus Lacupenus (A.D. 925) it was desired for political reasons that Simeon, Prince of Bulgaria, should die.   It was significant that at Constantinople there stood a column, associated with the life of Simeon in some way or other, and an astronomer told Romanus that if it was broken Simeon would perish. The head of the column was therefore struck off and it was afterwards learned that Simeon had died of heart failure at that precise moment.

To strike folk dead with thunder, to blind them with lightning, to scorch them by heat,

to freeze them with hail, to blight their crops,
to distemper their cattle, to poison their children—all these powers and more were supposed to lie within the circumference of the
witches' power.

These ideas were widely held to, and
among those that have made worthy mention of them is Allan Ramsay, author of *The
Gentle Shepherd*. Living at a time when witchcraft was very prevalent, especially in Scotland, he was able to speak with some authority, and those north of the Border especially
will appreciate his telling of the powers of the
witch in the following words :

> She can o'ercast the night, and cloud the moon,
> And mak the Deils obedient to her crune,
> At midnight hours o'er the kirkyards she raves,
> And howks unchristen'd weans out of their graves ;
> Boils up their livers in a warlock's pow,
> Rins witherskins about the hemlock's low ;
> And seven times does her prayers backwards pray ;
> Then mix't with venom of black taids and snakes.
> Of this unsousy pictures aft she makes
> Of ony ane she hates ;—and gars expire
> With shaw and racking pains afore a fire :
> Stuck full of pines the devilish pictures melt ;
> The pain by fowk they represent is felt.
> Whilst she and cat sit beeking in her yard, etc.

As though the foregoing catalogue of evils
were not enough to get along with, the

witches were credited with a good many
more, among which, as is mentioned in the
previous chapter, was the power of inflicting
sufferings and calamities of the most awful
kind upon both man and beast by " Overlooking " or " the Evil Eye."

Belief in the existence of the evil eye was
an acknowledgment that the possessors of it
were able to bewitch or even kill by a
glance.[1]   It was one of the most widespread
and venerable of human beliefs, accepted by
mediæval authors and fathers of the Church
and primitive races everywhere.

In more than one witch-trial it was confessed that Satan had told his disciples :
" If you bare ill-will to anybody, look on
them with open eyes, and pray evil for them
in my name and you will get your heart's
desires."

In Rome at one time it was so prevalent
that laws were passed to counter its evil.
Possession of the evil eye was said to be in-
voluntary : in some cases, however, it was
thought to be maliciously cultivated or deve-
loped under the impulse of envy.   When this
was known to be the case, its evil influence
could be counteracted by saying, or showing,

[1] Deuteronomy xxviii. 54.

something ridiculous or rude ; which, as one may readily imagine, led to all manner of performances. By those that were shy or conscientious the exhibition of an image or model accompanied by loud laughter was claimed sufficient.

On account of the uncertainty as to whether or no anyone was being overlooked it became the custom to abstain from verbal praise within anyone's hearing—for envy's sake. If a person was asked how he was in health, the reply would be of an evasive or non-committal character and therefore not subject to alteration by the envious possessor of the evil eye. To-day, if asked the same question, our subconscious self replies, "Not so bad" —and then we touch wood and whistle. In fact, we ridicule it, just as our ancestors did, without knowing it. That people did really and truly fall into a decline and waste away after having been glanced at is, of course, an accepted truth. Mediæval writers were wont to contrast the influence of the glance with the fascination of terror resembling paralysis of the whole nervous system, observed when serpents have had their eyes fixed upon their prey.

According to the author of *The Craven*

Glossary, published at the beginning of last century, it was possible in Yorkshire, at least, to kill a pear-tree by glancing at it with an evil eye. It appears a man possessed an evil eye and he knew it, but not wishing to harm any human being by letting its glance fall upon them, he " ivvry mornin' as soon as he first oppans the dowr fixes his een o' that pear tree, an it deed right away."

Only a few years ago a Lanarkshire farmer confessed to a friendly folklorist that " the eye " had caused a deal of mischief in his dairy, where a fellow about the farm had been sent away for misbehaving himself. His mother, in revenge, had overlooked his cows for a whole year so that his churns would not cream.

As probably the reader may wonder what happens when a person not inclined to witchcraft or the casting of spells finds himself unfortunately possessed of " a queer eye," we have the following story told by another folklorist, only about a score or so of years ago. He says that when a child he was considered to have what was called " a blink of an ill e'e," so an old lady " skilly " in such matters was brought to the house. The door was then locked, the possessor of the " ill e'e " seated in a chair, a good fire was made, and a borrowed saxpence was brought to light. A tablespoon was then filled with water, and the coin was used to scoop up as much salt as possible, which in turn was put in the spoon. Water and salt were then stirred with the forefinger until both were well mixed. With this liquid the soles of the feet and the palms of the hands were anointed three times : after each anointing the patient had to taste it. The wet forefinger was then drawn across the brow—this was known as " scoring aboon the breath." What remained of the liquid was then thrown into the fire with a " Guid preserve frae a' skaith." Recovery was supposed to follow.

To avert the influence of the evil eye, as has been mentioned elsewhere, many and numerous devices were adopted, and the " scoring aboon the breath " is a reminder of the " scoring above the mouth " treatment used with such brutality against the witches —a horseshoe being used for the purpose. In the *Edinburgh Annual Register* of 1814 mention is made of a shepherd who, having suspected an old woman living fifteen miles away of overlooking his cows, went to her residence with a horseshoe in his hand and scored her forehead so severely that she died.

Although the superstitions made mention of here are those in the main connected with witchcraft in Europe, the same superstitions, only slightly modified, have been, and still are, common to all primitive or backward people.

They have grown out of mankind's beliefs and sentiments towards the mysteries of nature—birth, life, sickness, death, and so on—and they may be regarded as natural reactions against forces and happenings little understood.

Primitive mankind, finding itself plagued with " evils " of one kind and another, had to devise some means whereby the evil could be overcome, and nothing appealed to it so much as the doing of those things which have come to be referred to simply as " magic " ; and, crude as much of it must appear to be, there is, at least in some of it, not a little of what must be confessed to be a semblance of real wisdom.

Take, for instance, the very primitive practice of " sympathetic magic," by which someone is made to suffer by being " touched," or another already suffering is made well by the means of incantations and " sympathy."

Why, here is the very foundation upon which has been built the science and art of mesmerism, hypnosis, and suggestion as a therapeutic quantity with, if you like, psycho-analysis thrown in ; and the faith healings of to-day are a development of the same old idea.

In unenlightened parts of the world disease and sickness are still regarded as the work of a wizard, and the treatment for recovery is made by another wizard who professes to take away from the sick person the object or " the cause " of the disease that had been placed there by the first wizard ! To-day, the chief part of the physician's work is not so much to supply medicine as to instil into the psycho-sick patient an assurance that the " cause " of the sickness has never been in existence at all, or if it has, it will certainly disappear by the taking of a little tonic ; or, in other words, his chief business, like that of the wizard, is to develop " the will to be well."

Where, in the bad old times, bodily disease was ascribed to possession by a spirit, the usual remedy was exorcism [1]—the black art

[1] An interesting instance of exorcism such as was commonly practised by the Jews in about the year 30

—a direct appeal to other spirits. When this failed to aid in driving out the devils that were already in the fortress, so to speak, the purifying power of fire was requisitioned. Thus the burning of witches was not so much for punishment as that it was thought to be efficacious as a purge.

If overlooking inflicted anyone with an evil spirit and sickness, then it was thought that the sickness, along with the evil spirit that caused it, could be transferred by " a wise man " or a witch-doctor to some object such as a tree, an animal, or even a stone. This has come to be known as Fetichism ; at one time, no doubt, practised in England, it is still in vogue in various parts of the world. Before the transference can possibly take place, however, the wizard or medicine-man must force the superior spirits to comply

is the following : Josephus, who attributed the invention to Solomon, tells how he, as an eye-witness, had seen a Jew named Eleazar casting out demons in the presence of Vespasian, Titus, their officers, and the army. His method was to draw the demon out through the nostrils by a ring and a particular root. Hereupon the man fell down, and Eleazar, with various incantations and in the name of Solomon, adjured the demon not to return. And then in proof that the cure was effectual, he put a basin of water a little way off and bade the demon, as he departed, to overturn it !

with his desires. To get this compliance the wizard gets possession of something belonging to the bewitched, such as the parings of the finger-nails, a lock of hair, a tooth, a piece of clothing, or some other old thing, and then the superior deities are helpless. With much incantation and noise the spirit causing the sickness is driven out, and at the word of command enters into just what it is told to enter, casual passers-by or wayside images [1] of various character being called into service. In some parts little men made of dough are placed by the roadside on purpose. The term Fetichism is probably elastic enough to allow it to be described to-day in the one word " substitution."

Mental illnesses were supposed to be caused

---

[1] The god Shaman, commonly referred to as the master of medical cures and prescriptions, and dating from about the year 1200 B.C., had his origin in a small clay figure resembling the familiar golliwog. As priest and medicine-man possessing magico-religious rites he was able to drive out demons from those that were diseased. To aid him in his work of healing he boasted of intimacy with all the spirits and a knowledge of the therapeutic value of herbs, etc. His cures took place amidst a deal of noise, and behaviour ecstatic in character. His clay image placed by the roadside possessed the added power of warding off pestilence and the assurance of a healthy spiritual existence in the kingdom of the blessed.

at times by the evil eye just in the same way as they were thought to be due to " unclean spirits " or " devils " entering through the cranium ; and the cure was thought to be brought about when a hole was made in the skull—trepanning—for the devils to escape through.

It is hardly believable, but until sixty years or so ago, in England lunacy was thought to be caused by " possession," and a wheel-like instrument was devised for use in mad-houses upon which the sufferer would be strapped, and the wheel when set revolving would go at such a terrific speed that the demons would come out and fly for their very existence.

Another idea that was supposed to give witches their opportunity for inflicting punishment and was believed to lead ghosts or other spiritual agents to send disease, was the breaking of a Taboo—the meaning of taboo being the recognition or performance of some recognised custom or observance. For example, it was the custom before the advent of motor-cars for superstitious people to wet their finger with spittle and mark a cross on their shoes when they saw a brown-

and-white horse. If they did not do it, they would break the taboo and would expect to get run over or something of the sort. To-day it is taboo not to lend an umbrella. If you do lend it, you break the taboo, and, incidentally, you lose the umbrella.

This transference of disease to trees and stones may seem queer indeed, but surely it is preferable to the custom which the folk of Lancashire had, or may still have, of getting rid of their warts. Their idea was to rub the wart with a pebble, then to put the pebble in a bag and drop it on the way to church. Whoever found the bag got the wart.

Apparently the idea lingers in other places besides, for a Cornish folklorist has stated how an old lady told him that on one occasion she unwittingly picked up such a bag, and sure enough, in a short time warts began to grow on her hands. Such is the power of an expectant or, if you like, anticipatory mind.

Just as illness, bad luck, and all the rest of our troubles were supposed to come, in the beginning, from either witches or devils, so it was thought that the power of healing was attributable to the gods. Eventually the idea became to be associated with what was called the divine right of kings. So that in the eleventh century, when Edward the Confessor, a very holy man, lay dying, he ordered that all those suffering from disease might be brought to him ; and touching them, they were healed. In this manner there came into being what is referred to in history as " the Royal Touch " : a cure for " King's Evil," or scrofula, or, as it is better known to-day, tuberculous glands.

After Edward's death, the performance, for a time, fell into disuse, but was restored by Henry II and perpetuated by Henry III and the three Edwards. In 1465 Henry VII dispensed with the actual " touching," but instead issued a small coin—the Golden Angel—to be worn round the neck to bring about a cure. This is referred to in literature as a " touchpiece," and it played a somewhat similar part as did the mascots which were worn as a protection against witchcraft.

The " Royal Touch " itself was revived by Queen Anne, and Dr. Johnson as a child was taken to her for treatment.

Under Charles I, Charles II, and James II the " touch " was greatly in vogue. Of Charles I it is said that as many as a hundred were " touched " by him in one day ; while Charles II is credited with having touched between seven and eight hundred, also in one day. Indeed, it became the fashion to be " touched," and thousands availed themselves of " the cure " whether they suffered or no. To many a person desirous of coming into close touch with royalty, scrofula was " the only way." In *The Tragedy of Macbeth* we are reminded how

> . . . strangely-visited people,
> All swol'n and ulcerous, pitiful to the eye,
> The mere despair of surgery, he cures,
> Hanging a golden stamp about their necks,
> Put on with holy prayers.

And in the hanging about the neck of the golden stamp and the prayers there was given a wonderful impetus to the use of those old mascots that were designed originally to frustrate the Evil Eye and other baneful influences.

This cure by " touch," as interesting as it be, is perhaps after all not so astounding as another kind of cure by touch—the touching of the dead ; modified on occasions by the touching of not only those that die natural deaths, but by the touching of hanged men. It was a common sight in London, not so many years ago, to see people who were evidently ill in mind as well as body being led up to the scaffold in Old Bailey so that the hand of a man just executed might be touched. Indeed, it became one of the sights, almost as much worth seeing, so it was considered, as the actual hanging ; and it has been affirmed that at Northampton sufferers from goitre used to gather round the gallows when an execution took place, and await their turn to ascend for the purpose of being healed. The executioner charged a small fee and then stroked the affected part with the dead man's hand. Even after the execution of Charles I chips of the block and grains of the bloodstained sand found ready purchasers among those who believed them to possess the power of healing.

Yet another mode of healing by touch was there, and just as efficacious—that of being touched by the hand of a suicide. Not so many years ago there was recorded in the *Folk-Lore Record* an account of how a woman suffering from an enlarged throat, and hearing that a boy had committed suicide by drowning, in Sussex, went there in all haste, and had the affected part stroked by the dead hand—"nine times from east to west, and then nine times from west to east."

Perhaps the most interesting of all accounts is the following, as it conjures up in the mind all manner of quaint possibilities. The account is to be found in the *Fairy Superstitions of Donegal*. At a wake in the wild region of Donegal, an old man, bent almost double and tottering slowly, supported by a staff, entered the house and sat down by the fire. He was a neighbour of the bereaved family, so that the people sitting round the hearth in the wake-house were not surprised to see him join them. The company, what with the smoke of their pipes and the smoke from the peat fire, was a very dismal one; it was the day of the funeral. The coffin had arrived, and the dead man was to be placed in it and carried to the lonely church-yard. Before they raised him from his couch, however, the old cripple-man crept over to where he lay, and taking the hand of the corpse in his, lifted it to his shoulder, arm, and leg in as grave manner as possible, saying as he did so, " Tak' my pains wi' you, Thady, in the name of God ! " The other folk present, stepping backward, whispered, " Poor old Donald ! poor crayther, he's sore afflicted wi' the pains, why shouldn't he try the cure ? " Again, when the coffin was being lifted over the threshold, Donald called after it, " Tak' my pains wi' you, Thady, in the name of God ! " That Thady *did* take away the pains is evident, for Donald was seen to walk away " as well as possible," leaving his stick behind him.

In these enlightened times we may smile at the idea of anyone ever believing in the power of the Evil Eye, but time was when it was as much a reality as the King's Touch. The fathers of the Early Church believed in it, and if you like you may read about it in early records by referring to Galatians iii. That people did really believe in its power there can be no gainsaying, and as they believed in it then it follows that it did all that it was supposed to do. If they came under its ban they were bewitched, and the best thing to do then was to do the proper thing, which was, according to tradition, to counteract the evil by an application of the black art. If this was not done, then the best thing to do was to admit of being a luckless wight, to put one's house in order, and to hope that the agony would not be prolonged.

Before complete resignation, however, one

or two other things could be tried as an antidote, the most popular of which was the
wearing of amulets or charms. We will just
call to mind some of the oldest here, and refer
to them again a few pages further on.

As the special form of evil supposed to be
flashed from one eye to another could be
thwarted or warded off by holding up the
hand for protection, so it came about that a
charm representing the hand came into existence. Proof has been given that these
charms were worn so far back in history as
500 to 1000 B.C.

Another charm was the early Egyptian
sacred scarab, dedicated to Khepera, a sun-
god. Pliny describes it as like the sun because its natural habit was to make pellets
of clay and roll them along : illustrating the
rolling along of the sun ; creator of life, therefore an antidote for death. Just as important a charm as that of the scarab was the
representation of the eye of Osiris. It was,
and still is in Egypt, used as the symbol of
courage, a protection from the evil eye, and
a giver of life.

Another, and the last to be mentioned here,
is the horseshoe. Nailed over a door it is
supposed to protect the inmates from the evil

eye in particular, and of witchcraft in general.
The horns from it must point upwards, not
only because the luck will run out if it is the
other way, but because if the points hang
downwards it will not represent the symbol of
Diana, the Moon Goddess. Besides, one never
saw the new moon of which it is a representation upside down unless . . . !

That fear, and even death, should occur
on account of belief in the evil power of
fascination, although at first seemingly ridiculous, is not really so difficult a task to a
mind in harmony with the idea of dying as
some folk might imagine.

Not so many hundreds of years ago the
superstitious Irish peasantry attributed to
their bards the power " to rime either man
or beast to death."[1] This is accounted for
by the great dread in which the Irish peasants
held their bards, regarding them as a priestly
caste.[2] In Irish literature the power of the
Irish satirists to rime men to death is frequently referred to, and is the subject of
various ancient legends.

Shakespeare had evidently heard of it, and

[1] Scot's *Discoverie of Witchcraft* (1584).
[2] Spenser's *View of Present State of Ireland* (1595).

perhaps believed it, for he referred to it as
" rhyming Irish rats to death."[1]

Some people have even been known to
possess what has been called " dying at
will," and Dr. Cheyne, an eighteenth-century
physician and a relative to Bishop Burnet,
gives the following account of such a case
in his book on *Hypochondriacal Distempers*.
The doctor with two others was away on
holiday when " Colonel Townshend, a gentleman of excellent natural parts, and of
great honour and integrity, sent for us early
one morning ; we waited on him . . . we
found his senses clear, and his mind calm, his
nurse and several servants were about him.
He had made his will and settled his affairs.
He told us he had sent for us to give him
some account of an odd sensation he had for
some time observed and felt in himself ;
which was, that composing himself, he could
die or expire when he pleased, and yet by an
effort, or somehow, he could come to life
again ; which, it seems, he had sometimes
tried before he sent for us. We heard this
with surprise ; but as it was not to be accounted for from now common principles,
we could hardly believe the fact as he related

[1] Shakespeare's *As You Like It*.

it, much less give any account of it ; unless he
should please to make the experiment before
us, which we were unwilling he should do, lest,
in his weak condition, he might carry it too
far. He continued to talk very distinctly and
sensibly above a quarter of an hour about
this surprising sensation, and insisted so much
on our seeing the trial made, that we were at
last forced to comply. We all three felt his
pulse first ; it was distinct, though small and
thready ; and his heart had its usual beating.
He composed himself on his back, and lay in
a still posture some time ; while I held his
right hand, Dr. Baynard laid his hand on his
heart, and Mr. Skrine held a clean looking-
glass to his mouth. I found his pulse sink
gradually, till at last I could not feel any by
the most exact and nice touch. Dr. Baynard
could not feel the least motion in his heart,
nor Mr. Skrine the least soil of breath in the
bright mirror he held to his mouth ; then
each of us by turns examined his arm, heart,
and breath, but could not by the nicest
scrutiny discover the least symptom of life
in him. We reasoned a long time about this
odd appearance as well as we could, and all
of us judged it inexplicable, and finding he
still continued in that condition we began to

conclude that he had indeed carried the experiment too far, and at last were satisfied he was actually dead, and were just ready to leave him. This continued about half an hour by nine o'clock in the morning in autumn. As we were going away, we observed some motion about the body, and upon examination found his pulse and the motion of his heart gradually returning; he began to breathe gently, and speak softly; we were all astonished to the last degree at this unexpected change, and after some further conversation with him, and among ourselves, went away fully satisfied as to all the particulars of this fact, but confounded and puzzled, and not able to form any rational scheme that might account for it. He afterwards called for his Attorney, added a Codicil to his Will, settled legacies on his servants, received the Sacrament, and calmly and composedly expired about five or six o'clock that evening. . . . I have narrated the facts, as I saw and observed them deliberately and distinctly, and shall leave to the philosophic reader to make what inference he thinks fit; the Truth of the material circumstances I will warrant."

So you see, if people thought they were

going to die because they were bewitched, they simply helped the prognostication to come true, and found the dying no more difficult than did the Hon. Colonel Townshend.

Fear of death from other things besides witchcraft is just as deadly, and many instances could be quoted in which fancy has played strange tricks. Even to-day, just as people living in the primitive places of the earth break up a settlement when a death occurs in it, so there are people of education and refinement who will not continue to live in a house in which there has been a death. And if there is knowledge of the death having been the result of cancer or something of the sort, the fearful mind easily imagines a repetition or even a transference of the suffering.

In Chicago as late as 1875 the body of a woman who had died of consumption was taken out of the grave and the lungs burned, because her relatives thought she was drawing them after her. Another incident is authoritatively given in which a resident of Rhode Island had the dead body of his daughter taken out of her grave and the heart burned on account of an idea in the family that it was wasting away the lives of others.

In Devonshire to this day it is believed that

if hair of a dead man is buried under a house those that live there will always be subject to fevers ; while in parts of Ireland it is believed that dead men buried near a house will in the night pinch those that live in the adjacent houses—"dead men's pinches" they call it—and to prove the assertion they will (depending upon where the pinch happens to have been) show you the discoloured marks on the skin resembling the pinches or bruises which they have begotten in so mysterious a fashion.

In the next chapter will be given a few narratives showing how the spell worked in some notable instances of practical witchcraft.

CHAPTER IV

PRACTICAL WITCHCRAFT

IN the previous chapter mention has been made of the witches using small models for the purpose of torture. As the witches were known to use these trumperies, and as the superstitions connected with them were explicitly believed in by the malicious intellectuals as well as by the ignorant, woe betide anyone in possession of a lead, wax, or composition model, or for that matter an ornament of any description, on which suspicion of witchcraft or spell-casting could be cast, or a charge based.

An early account of a witch-trial of some importance in which these images figured is as follows :—

In 1441, Roger Bolinbroake, an astronomer, and Thomas Southwell, a canon of St. Stephen's Chapel, Westminster, were arrested on a charge of conspiring against the life of the king, Henry VI. The manner of the conspiracy was, that Roger *should labour to*

consume the king's person by necromancie,
and that Thomas should *say masses upon
certain instruments with which the said Roger
should exercise his witchcraft,* meaning to use
models of the victims made of wax or lead.

On being examined before the King's
Council, Roger Bolinbroake with adamite
servility declared that the necromancies
were wrought at the instigation of Dame
Eleanor, daughter of Lord Cobham; and so
it came about that the lady was then commanded to appear at Westminster before the
Archbishops of Canterbury and York, and
the Bishops of Salisbury and Winchester, to
answer charges of necromancy, witchcraft,
heresy, and treason. The result of the examination was that the lady had to do penance,
after imprisonment in a castle in Kent;
Bolinbroake and Southwell in turn having
their heels bruised by being sent to the Tower
of London.

On a November morning, four months
after her arrest, the said Eleanor was made
to walk from the Temple Stairs, along the
Strand and Fleet Street, to St. Paul's, carrying a two-pound wax taper in her hand, by
way of penance. Two days later she was
compelled to do penance from Old Swan Steps

in Thames Street, through Gracechurch Street to Aldgate Church, and then, after another day or two, from Queenhithe, through Cheapside, to St. Michael's Church, in Cornhill; then she was sent away to end her days in Kenilworth Castle.

Meanwhile, Thomas Southwell, the canon, had died in the Tower. Bolinbroake, having taken his trial at the Guildhall of London, had been condemned to death; and so, with little consideration as to his comfort, he was fastened upon a hurdle and drawn at the horse's tail [1] through mud and mire from the Tower, along Chepe, past St. Paul's, across Holborn Valley and the Fleet Ditch, to St. Giles-in-the-Fields, and then to Tyburn, where he was ceremoniously hanged, and then quartered.

Margery Goodmayne, of Westminster, a reputed witch, to whom Dame Eleanor was said to have resorted, and of whose " sorcerie and witchcraft " she was accused of using, was taken to Smithfield, tied to a post, and, with the brutality of the period, burned.

[1] This fate of riding on a hurdle drawn at a horse's tail was also, as will be remembered, meted out to the bakers of London if they gave short weight.

In old documents, historical and otherwise, there are to be found many other references to the artifices of witchcraft. The following, concerning such high personages as King Edward IV and Richard III, particulars of which are furnished in the Rolls of Parliament, will no doubt be of interest. They are, of course, written in Old English; but will be no less interesting for that matter.

Contemporary pamphlets telling out the same story are existent, and although they bear no imprint it is probable that they were printed by the redoubtable Caxton in the press set up by him at Westminster. Strangely enough, Caxton's patron was Earl Rivers, a brother-in-law of Edward IV, who figures in the narrative.

The charge is against the Duchess of Bedford for intriguing with a certain Thomas Wake to "fix the king's love" upon her daughter Elizabeth by means of witchcraft and the black art. This Elizabeth eventually became the wife of Edward IV, and mother of the unfortunate princes whom Richard, according to our school books, caused to be murdered in the Tower of London.

The document reads as follows:

"Edward by the grace of God, kyng of

Englond and of Fraunce, and lord of Irland, to the reverend fader in God Robert byshope of Bathe and Wells, oure chaunceller, greting. Forasmoche as we send unto you within these oure lettres the tenure of an acte of oure grete counsaill, callid the parliment-chambre, within the kyngs paleis att Westminster, the x day of Februarie, the ixth yere of the regne of oure soveraygne lord the kyng Edward the IIIIth, in the presence of the same oure soveraigne lord, and my lordis of his grete counsail, whos names ben under writen, a supplicacion addressed unto oure said soveraygne lord, on the behalf of the high and noble princesse Jaquet duchesse of Bedford. . . .

" To the kyng oure soveraygne lord : shewith and lamentably complayneth unto your highness your humble and true liegewoman Jaquet duchesse of Bedford, late the wyf of your true and faithfull knyght and liegeman Richard late erle of Ryvers, that where shee at all tyme hath, and yit doth, treuly beleve on God accordyng to the feith of Holy Chirche, as a true cristen woman oughth to doo, yet Thomas Wake squier, contrarie to the lawe of God, lawe of this land, and all reason and good consciens, caused her to be brought in

a commune noyse and disclaundre of wyche-
craft thorouout a grete part of this youre
reaume, surmything that she shuld have usid
wichecraft and sorcerie, insomuch as the said
Wake caused to be brought to Warrewyk
atte youre last beyng there, soveraigne lord,
to dyvers of the lords thenne beyng ther
present, *a image of lede made lyke a man of
armes, conteyning the lengthe of a mannes fynger,
and broken in the myddes,* and made fast with
a wyre, sayying that it was made by your
said oratrice to use with the said wichcraft
and sorsory." . . .

This first charge broke down, but was
revived in an interesting form after Edward
IV's death. Included in it was the statement
that the marriage of Edward and Elizabeth
was made by sorcery and witchcraft :

" Over this, amonges other things, more
specially wee consider howe that, the tyme
of the reigne of kyng Edward the iiiith, late
deceased, after the ungracious pretensed
marriage, as all England hath cause soo to say,
made betwixt the said king Edward and
Elizabeth sometyme wife to sir John Grey
knight, late nameing herself and many years
heretofore quene of Englond, the order of all
poletique rule was preverted, the lawes of

God and of Gods church, and also the lawes
of nature and of Englond, and also the laudable customes and liberties of the same,
wherein every Englishman is inheritor, broken,
subverted, and contempred, against all reason
and justice, soo that this land was ruled by
selfewill, and pleasure, feare, and drede, all
manner of equite and lawes layd apart and
despised, whereof ensued many inconvenients
and mischiefs, as murdres, extorsions, and
oppressions ; namely, of poore and impotent
people, soo that no man was sure of his lif,
land, ne lyrelode, ne of his wif, doughter, ne
servaunt, every good maiden and woman
standing in drede to be ravished and defouled.
And besides this, what discords, inward
battailles, effasion of christian mens blode,
and namely by the destruction of the noble
blode of this londe, was had and comitted
within the same, it is evident and notarie
thourough all this reame, unto the great sorowe
and hevynesse of all true Englishmen. And
here also we considre, howe that *the seid
pretensed mariage betwixt the abovenamed king
Edward and Elizabeth Grey was made of grete
presumption, without the knowyng and assent
of the lords of this lond, and also by sorcerie and
wichecrafte*, committed by the said Elizabeth

and her moder Jaquett duchesse of Bedford, as the common opinion of the people, and the public voice and fame is thorough all this land; and hereafter, if and as the caus shall require, shall bee proved sufficiently in tyme and place convenient. And here also we consider, howe that the said pretensed marriage was made privatly and secretely, without edition of banns, in a private chambre, a prophare place, and not openly in the face of the churche, aftre the lawe of Goddes churche, but contrarie thereunto, and the laudable custome of the churche of Englonde. And howe, also, that at the tyme of contract of the same pretensed marriage, and bifore and longe tyme after, the said king Edward was and stode maryed and trouth-plight to oone dame Elianor Butteler, doughter of the old earle of Shrewesbury, with whome the same king Edward had made a precontract of matrimonie, long tyme bifore he made the said pretensed marriage with the said Elizabeth Grey, in manner and fourme abovesaid. Which premisses being true, as in veray trouth they been true, it appeareth and followeth evidently that the said king Edward duryng his lif, and the seid Elizabeth, lived together sinfully and dampnably in adultery, against the lawe of God and of his churche ; and therefore noo marvaile that, the souverain lord and the head of this land being of such ungodly disposicion, and provokyng the ire and indignacion of oure Lord God, such haynous mischieffs, and inconvenients, as is above remembred, were used and comitted in the reaume among the subjects. Also it appeareth evidently and followeth that all thissue and children of the said king Edward been bastards, and unable to inherite or to clayme any thing by inheritance by the lawe and custome of Englond."

It was in this manner that Richard, Duke of Gloucester, was able to pose as the defender of the law and religion against the " evil and lawless conduct " of Edward IV and the princes who were " born through the agency of sorcery and witchcraft."

Thus the belief in the power of witchcraft flowed on in a deep undercurrent of superstition. It was believed in by the people, feared by the Church, and used by the Crown to further its own ends, until it became a kind of vendetta against which there was no real security, and from which there was little chance of escape after once having become suspect.[1]

Another account worth mentioning here is that concerning Jane Shore, of whom many a love-story has been written at one time or another.

Jane Shore, as the reader perhaps knows, was the beautiful, though unfortunate, mistress of Edward IV. Little is known of her early years. She is said to have been the daughter of a London citizen, and to have been married to a Lombard Street jeweller who afterwards left her upon hearing that the king had become her paramour.

After Edward's death she became attached to Lord Hastings, and by espousing the cause of the young princes roused the anger of Richard III. A charge of witchcraft was then brought against both of them by Richard, as being the surest means of ridding himself of their opposition. To be brief, Hastings lost his head over the affair—in more senses than

[1] One of the excuses of Henry VIII for sending Anne Boleyn to the Tower was, that he *" had been seduced by witchcraft on the occasion of his marriage, which, therefore, was null and void,"* and also *" because God would not permit them to have issue."*

one—and Jane Shore was committed to the Tower.

After a trial, in which she made a defence so excellent as to confuse her judges and accusers, she was handed over to the considerate care of the ecclesiastics, who forthwith ordered her to do penance at St. Paul's. Clad only in a white kilt, she was led from the Bishop's Palace through the streets, the procession being headed by the bishop himself. Then, before St. Paul's Cross—the site of which may to this day be seen at the Cannon Street corner, inside the Churchyard railings—she stood, taper in hand, to make her confession. Holinshed, the old chronicler, has very beautifully recorded how " In her penance she went, in countenance and pace demure, so womanlie, that albeit she was out of all raiment save her kertle onlie, yet went she so faire and lovelie, namelie, while the wondering of the people cast a comelie blush in her cheeks, that her great shame won her much praise among those that were more amorous of her bodie than curious of her soule. And many good folks that hated her living, yet pitied they more her penance than rejoiced therein, when they considered that the Protector procured it more of a

corrupt intent than any virtuous affection."
Her home, her fortune, and all she possessed,
were then seized by the order of the " Protector," Richard. Reduced to the direst
poverty and deserted by all whom she had
helped in her prosperity, she lived on, penuri-
ously, until the time of Henry VIII.

Years afterwards Sir Thomas More mentions her in quite felicitous terms, and observes
that, although time and affliction had destroyed her personal charms, she yet retained
to the last that gentleness of manner which
had conspired to enslave a monarch's heart.
The culminating tragedy in the life of this
gallant woman, of whom so many love-ballads
have been sung, was her lonely death in a
ditch under the shadow of the old London
Wall near Bishopsgate—the ditch which is
said to have given rise to the commercial
thoroughfare known to all Jewry and most
of Christendom to-day as Houndsditch.

Truth is stranger than fiction, and so for
the sequel to the foregoing. After Jane
Shore had endured penance at the Cross of
St. Paul's, a servile preacher of Richard's
day, by name Dr. Shawe, addressed the
concourse of people that had gathered there

with regard to the "illegitimate" children
of Edward IV, and to recommend to their
affections instead the "legitimate Richard
as the express image of his father." This
was clever electioneering work—pardon the
reflection—but people evidently were not to
be wooed in this fashion, for when Richard
made his appearance directly Dr. Shawe had
said what he desired, " he witnessed only the
sullen silence of the spectators," after which,
as Stow says, " the preacher gat him home,
and never after durst go out for shame, but
kept out of sight like an owle ; and when he
once asked one that had been his olde friende
what the people talked of him, albeit that
his own conscience well shewed him that
they talked no good, yet when the other
answered him, that there was in every man's
mouth spoken of him much shame, it so struck
him to the heart, that in a few days after, he
withered, and consumed away ! "

A famous trial contemporary with the foregoing, in which wax images used in the practice
of the Black Art has figured, was that brought
against Lady Fowlis in Scotland. The evidence was, that with the aid of witchcraft,
images, and poisons, she had endeavoured to

kill several persons who happened to stand in the way of her ambitions, one of which ambitions was to marry her daughter to the then Laird of Balnagown. As the Laird was already married, she conceived the brilliant idea of killing off the Laird's young wife, together with two other members of the family; and for the purpose she consulted some old hags familiar with the art of poisoning and the making of images.

Dishes were then poisoned and models representing the intended victims were deftly shaped; these models were hung up and shot at with elf-arrows—small arrows having sharp flints at their points.[1] As the images were pierced by the arrows, so the Laird's wife and others whom they symbolised were said to have endured much suffering.

Through some deceit or disagreement between the old hags and the lady there was a quarrel, which in turn was followed by a confession and a giving away of all the secrets.

---

[1] The stone arrowheads of our ancestors that are occasionally picked up in country places are to this day commonly referred to by the old people as " elfshots." Stories are even told of how farmer So-and-so's cattle fell ill and died after having had these things shot at them by the fairies.

Her ladyship's dark intentions were exposed, her designs frustrated, and she herself brought to trial.

As this last illustration is from Scottish story, there naturally comes to mind the most familiar of all the witchcraft charges —that of Lady Glamis, executed in 1537 as a member of the rebel House of Douglas conspiring to bring back to power her brother, Earl of Angus, from exile. The narrative is so well known that there is little need to retell it.

Witch-hunting and witch-trial procedure in Scotland in the sixteenth century was by examination before Minister and Kirk Session of the parish; trial taking place by their appeal to the Privy Council. Then special commissioners were appointed by Privy Council; but the juries were horribly biased, and evidence by torture was permissible. The death penalty was imposed on proof of " witchcraft, sorcery, and necromancy."

Another noted Scottish witch-trial was that in connection with a charge brought against John Stuart, Master of Orkney, in June, 1596, on the count that he had visited a witch to ask her aid and help in poisoning his brother, the Earl of Orkney. The notorious witch (all

witches were described as " notorious ") was
Alysoun Balfour. Her husband, her son and
her daughter were all implicated.

After the arrest of the family, Mrs. Balfour
was put in what was known as " the warm
hose " ; that is, a kind of iron stocking made
to open down the centre and to clamp on the
legs. To extort confession a movable fur-
nace would be brought and the leg placed
in it, confession invariably being made
according to the degree of suffering involved.
The woman's husband, an old man of eighty-
one, was in the " long-irons " or shackles,
weighing some hundredweight. Her son
was in " the boots," a barbarous instrument
of torture used for crushing the foot, every
time it was hit with a mallet—the punishment in this case was fifty-seven strokes.
And her little daughter, aged seven, had
the " thumbscrew " properly and carefully
adjusted.

They all confessed as the pain increased
in intensity, but recanted so soon as the torture
was removed.

In this particular case the " Assisa " before
whom they were tried were considerate enough
to condemn only Mrs. Balfour. So she was
burned on Castle Hill at Christmas, 1596. (In

one other rare case where the "Assisa" would not pronounce a verdict of guilt they had a sharp reprimand from King James, asking for an explanation ; which explanation, either from the manner in which it was given or for its contents, resulted in the majority of the jury being tried for wilful error of assize.)

Thomas Palpla, a servant of the Balfour family just mentioned, was arrested for goodness knows what, and kept for eleven days and nights in the " caspie-claws "—a spikey instrument for fastening on the limbs; also during that time at intervals of twice a day he was stripped of his clothing and " scourged in sic soirt that they left nather flesch nor hyde vpoun hym." He confessed and recanted so many times during the eleven days' trial that complete record as to what his final condition of mind was has not been stated. But, poor fellow ! whatever it was, the eleven days of conflict show very clearly that he was no coward, and in the end, like others born to a better purpose, his funeral pile lit up, blood-red, the sky o'er Castle Hill.

If Edinburgh had its bonfires, so had Aberdeen. In the year 1596 no less than twenty-three women were burned there as witches. In February of the following year Aberdeen paid away the sum of two pounds thirteen shillings and fourpence, being expenses incurred for the purchase of " peattis, tar-barrelis, fir, and coallis " necessary in the burning of a man named Thomas Lewis; whilst another payment soon afterwards was for eleven pounds odd for tar, etc., with an extra ten shillings for the trailing of one of the witches through the streets of the town in a cart, and then burying her—because she had cheated them by committing suicide in her cell !

What a lot of haggis that money would have purchased !

In Scotland the last execution for witchcraft was in 1722, and the last conviction five years later ; but illegal popular reprisals continued for long afterwards.

CHAPTER V

WITCHCRAFT ON THE CONTINENT

ALTHOUGH it was not at first intended to deal in this book with witchcraft other than as it appeared in England, it has been found to be irresistibly impossible to refrain from giving at least a kind of skeleton outline of its career on the continent of Europe; for it was, without doubt, the outbreaks of witch-mania abroad, with their terrible aftermath of persecution and horror, that gave contemporary outbreaks in England such a fearful impetus. The story of witchcraft in England will be continued a chapter or two farther on. It will be understood all the better for the interlude.

Up to the thirteenth century witchcraft on the Continent was treated as witchcraft pure and simple. Then, at the time of the Inquisition, it became confused with charges of heresy.

The Inquisition, as the reader will remember, was established in 1233 by the setting up in every parish of a priest and several laymen empowered to search for those that practised false doctrines and bring them before the bishops for trial and punishment. The bishops, however, soon tiring of the task, transferred the responsibility to the Dominicans.

Its tribunal was called the Holy Office or the Holy Inquisition. Its judges in their zeal encouraged informers, and concealed their names from those accused. Torture of a terrible description was used to extract evidence and confession. The attitude of the Church towards " false doctrine " was that divinations and sorcery and practices harmful to property were left to the secular authorities ; the church courts and the Inquisition concerned themselves only with the witches' doctrines that smacked of heresy, compact with the devil, abjuration of the faith of their baptism, and breach of clerical celibacy. The most notorious heretics were the Alpine peasants called the Waldenses or Vaudois, and from them all sorts of heresy and witchcraft were loosely but popularly called " Vauderie," just as we might now call any sort of discontent Bolshevism.

The Dominican black friars were organised

primarily to combat heresy, but as heresy and witchcraft were closely associated in the popular mind, we find sporadic outbreaks of persecution during the next two centuries, and especially in those areas which were most infected with heretical teaching.

The decree of Pope Innocent VIII carefully enumerated the heretical doctrines and unchristian practices of witchcraft, and commanded the Inquisitors of the Waldenses in Piedmont to summon before them all those " suspected of intrigue with the Devil," and invested them with power to punish as they thought fitting to the occasion ; with the result, that a persecution of heretics or witches became rife all over the Continent.

Upon charges of " divination, sorcery, and practices harmful to property " the witches were brought before the secular courts ; and upon the other, " compact with the Devil," they were brought before the Inquisitors. So they had very little chance of escaping.

On the Continent the charge of heresy meant torture, confession of false doctrine, and then death. That it was understood very differently in England is shown by the following. In 1372, a man alleged to have practised it, and with the head of a corpse and a book of magic in his possession as proof, was charged before the King's Bench at Southwark. The court, although acknowledging it to be a deed deserving of death if committed abroad, made it clear that as sorcery it was no indictment so far as the English law was concerned. The man was acquitted, but his book of magic and the skull were burned by the public executioner at Tothill Fields.

Thus it was in the thirteenth century that heresies and charges of witchcraft became prevalent on the Continent, and it was in the same century that the friar Stephen of Bourbon wrote the first descriptions of the witches' Sabbath. A century later it was followed by a Latin book, *The Hammer of the Witches*, written by two Inquisitors, the friars Sprenger and Institor, and published with the approval of the University of Cologne. Nothing original was claimed for this work, but it proved the actual existence of witchcraft with the usual clerical evidence, and gave the time-honoured rules for discovering it ; finally, it outlined the method of procedure in the civil and ecclesiastical courts. Its importance is due to the fact that it was the first book of its kind to be printed, and in consequence it came to be adopted far and wide as a handbook for witch-hunters.

For considerably over two hundred years after the setting up of the Inquisition there was a continuance of tortures, burnings and other horrors.

With such persistency was the decree of the Pope prosecuted that in Geneva alone, in three months, in the year 1515, so it is estimated by Delrio, nearly five hundred " witches " were condemned to death, while in the Diocese of Como a thousand paid the penalty in less than a year.

Some sixty years afterwards, from 1575, there were nine hundred condemned in fifteen years in Lorraine. It is also reckoned that in France during the reign of Henry III the executions must be numbered at about thirty thousand.

In Germany the tragedy was just as bad, especially during the religious wars following on the Reformation. In 1627, in Wurtzburg alone no fewer than one hundred and fifty-seven women, men, and young persons were burned to death in twenty-nine conflagrations. Hauber relates that among the victims there figured fourteen vicars of the Church, a blind girl, and number-

less children of ages between nine and twelve.
In another small district, that of Lindheim,
where the population was only about six
hundred, some thirty of them a year, for the
four years 1660–64, were put to death. Think
of it! Twenty per cent. of the population!

It is reckoned that in Germany between
the years 1610 and 1660 there were over one
hundred thousand convictions. So hardened
had the people become in the course of a
generation or two to the exhibitions of torture
that, except when their own kith and kin
were concerned, they raised little or no protest.

In 1728, at Szegedin, in Hungary, no fewer
than thirteen persons were burned alive
simultaneously, in three piles, amid horrors
of appalling cruelty.

Such callous depravity was there exhibited
on these occasions, that after a grand round-
up and burning of witches in Franconia and
Bamberg, the ballad-singers amused the crowd
by singing doggerel verses detailing how the
poor victims had sold themselves to the Devil.
The ballad was entitled *Druten Zeitung* (The
Witches' Chronicle), and sung to the tune of
"Dorothea." The printed account was fully
illustrated with woodcuts, showing with
hideous glee some pugilistic-looking devils

dragging into what was supposed to depict the confines of Hell as many creatures as they could clutch.

On the Continent, as in England, the most astonishing thing about the charge of sorcery and witchcraft was the simplicity of the whole business; for on occasions when a charge broke down, and with the release of the person accused there voluntarily came forward others who were quite willing, aye, even anxious, to play their part in the tragedy, and to die as martyrs for the cause. (Some explanations regarding the strange fantasy which led to these confessions will be found in a later chapter.) It was also surprisingly common at the trials for those accused to avow their guilt, and to confess how they had abjured Jesus Christ, had been initiated into the mysteries of the black art, had been baptised in the Devil's name, and had entered into an infernal compact with him for doing all manner of evil; and how they had, with the Devil's help, bewitched, poisoned, blighted, and tortured by means of arrows and images almost everything and everybody they were capable of thinking of.

Another astounding thing was the indiffer-

ence with which they would at times face
their accusers and voluntarily perjure themselves before their judges. For instance, in
1669, at Mora, in Sweden, there was a persecution of witches, and at the trials there
were as many as seventy-two women of
varying ages that confessed to having been
in the habit of meeting with others at a
place called Blocula, and that their gatherings
were frequently visited by the Devil if they
called for him loud enough: " Beelzebub,
come forth ! "

They also added the information that when
he did appear he " wore a red beard and
breeches to match, a grey coat and stock-
ings, and a peaked cap with cocks' feathers
in it " ; that he fed them with witch-butter
which made them sickly, and that sons and
daughters were born to him by the witches.
They said, in addition, that they had all been
baptised with a new name, which had been
written in blood in a big black book ; that
they had been given power to ride through
the air on broomsticks and horses called
" nightmares," and in this manner had carried
off children for the Devil's broth-pot—and
much more trumpery of a like nature.

The one little bit of humour about the

foregoing confession, not yet mentioned, was
the habit which Beelzebub had of closing
these little " at homes " by making the old
hags fly round and round him very many
times on their brooms until they became
dizzy. This seemed to have a somnolent
effect upon him, for he would fall asleep ;
but when he woke he would take the sticks
away from them and, in exchange, thrash
them soundly.

Apparently there were three places in
particular that the Continental witches were
in the habit of visiting when on flight. One
was the Brocken in Germany, an oak tree
near Benevento in Italy, and some place
unknown but according to all accounts beyond the Jordan. Their Sabbaths, like those
of other witches, were usually held on a
Thursday, and the Devil would be there in
the form of a goat or dog. The Sabbath
ceremony was opened in mock fashion by the
chief, who would read out the witches' com-
mandments. Then he would preach to them,
telling them that they were all his, and that
they had no soul whatsoever (for it had been
surrendered when they had given up their
names).

The whole service undoubtedly was one of

negatived Christianity. These night-flying escapades, it is of interest to note, were regarded by the clericals simply as fiction, but they renounced as heretics those that confessed that they believed in the reality of the illusion. In time, the final test as to whether those accused were witches or not rested upon evidence concerning the midnight flights; and strange as it may seem, judge and victim found it quite easy by mutual assistance to build up a coherent story of the abandonment to Satan. The stories became so universal and so complete in detail that they could not be rejected without discrediting the whole structure of witchcraft.

When the judges had it explained to them in one instance that the Devil, clever though he be, could not make a body fly through a closed door, they replied, "No! but he could create the illusion, and that was just as bad—it was heresy."

Not that this view of the belief in night-flying was new to the twelfth century. In the ninth it had been protested against, as is shown by the following pronouncement of the Church:

" Some wicked women, reverting to Satan, and seduced by the illusions and phantasms

of demons, believe and profess that they ride
at night with Diana on certain beasts, obey-
ing her commands as their mistress. Priests,
therefore, should preach that they know this
to be false, and that such phantasms are sent
by evil spirits, and he who believes such
things has lost his faith, and he who has
lost his faith is not of God, but of the Devil."
Thus it was then treated as a diabolical
illusion.

Another item of interest showing the anti-
Christian character of these gatherings and
flight was that if the name of Christ was
mentioned during the flight the one who
uttered it would fall to the earth. All these
illusions, as mad as they undoubtedly were,
were made the basis of charges under which
thousands of women were committed to the
flames.

Probably all the accounts on record are
emanations from a type of mind given more
to fanciful imaginings than to the recording
of actualities. There was the notorious case
of the Angel de la Barthe, for instance,
who at Toulouse in the year 1275 confessed
to having had habitual intercourse with
Satan, and who at the age of fifty-four had
borne a monster son possessing a wolf's

head and a devil's tail, and which for its
first two years was sustained on the flesh of
babes.

One of the most remarkable confessions—
not of night-flying particularly, but of mischievous witchcraft—was that of Marie
Renata, a sub-prioress at one time at the
Untezell Convent, near Wurtzburg.

Being initiated secretly into the mysteries
of witchcraft at the age of seventeen, she,
two years afterwards, against her wish, but
to please her guardians, entered a convent.
There, with pretended piety and an attention
to discipline, she won favour and in course of
time became sub-prioress, and would even
have been promoted still further had she
not at an unguarded moment shown her
real self by expressing in no uncertain manner
a decided disgust with the convent and
everybody connected with it. She had
now been at the convent for forty years,
and during the whole time had kept her
witchcraft propensities a secret, although
she had managed to work spasmodic but
studied spells of mischief, such as that of
mixing herbs with the food of the nuns and
causing them to have strange seizures in

consequence, and to suffer deliriums from which some did not recover.

From long security she at last became careless; and as the desire for stronger excitement made itself felt, so she lessened her vigilance and increased the risk when displaying her questionable talents. Her favourite tricks were to pass at night into the dormitories, making weird uncanny noises; or to utter loud shrieks from behind the convent wall; or, when the nuns were asleep, to creep quietly into their rooms and pinch them, or give them a stinger on their *pars posterior* with a strap carried especially for the purpose.

Such happenings, as one may readily imagine, caused much consternation and not a little indignation on the part of those who had been victimised, and, such is life, in the morning the *most* indignant of them all was the hypocritical sub-prioress!

Her undoing, however, was the possession of one of those beautifying appendages popularly referred to as "a lovely black eye," given to her one night when she was up to her tricks in the dormitory, and which she could not get rid of by breakfast-time. A confession made a little later by one of the nuns who lay dying—that Marie was

" uncanny," and that she had been tormented
by her in the night—also helped in the discovery. This dying confession caused some
alarm, and especially so when it was added
to by another nun becoming hysterical, or
" possessed " as it was styled, and telling of
unpardonable things that had been done by
her superior.

With adroitness worthy of a better cause,
the sub-prioress put the accusations down as
due to an imaginative mind, calumny, or
spitefulness, and so cleverly too that for a
time she played off to some extent any
further suspicions.

Then came a day when as many as five of
the nuns were caused to have strange seizures
simultaneously. When they recovered and
made charges against Marie, the superior
thought it serious enough to warrant deep
investigation, and the result was the placing
of the prioress in a cell. Here, realising that
she had been found out, she made confession
and avowed herself a witch.

For fear of scandal the superiors endeavoured to keep the affair a secret, and
with a hope of reforming her she was sent
away to a remote convent. But under her
old assumed piety she commenced her be-

witchings afresh, and with such success that many nuns had seizures even more severe than the last : so she was handed over to the civil authorities to be taken care of.

At the trial she repeated her belief in her bewitchment, and added that she had often been carried off by night to a witches' Sabbath, where she had been presented to Beelzebub in the usual fashion after abjuring God and the Virgin. Her real name had been changed to " Devil's Spawn," or something of that sort, and in the usual manner had been written by the Evil One in his black book ; while she herself had been branded on the body as the Devil's property. She believed all this, and, like other witches, more besides. Her trial found her " guilty," and she was condemned to be burnt ; but as she was seventy years of age, her judges gave her what they considered to be leniency in ordering that her head be struck off by the executioner before she was burnt.

Apart from the fantasies indulged in by many of those who believed themselves to be witches, the most terrible thing about witchcraft was, that when once a man, woman, or child had been accused of it there was very little chance of anything happening other than an execution, no matter how innocent they may have been.

At Lindheim on one occasion, six women were charged with having opened a grave and robbed it of the body of an unbaptised infant for the purpose of making a witch-broth. It so happened that these women were quite innocent of the charge, and, to prove it, the husband of one applied for an official examination of the grave. This was granted, and the condition of the coffin definitely disproved the charge. But the severe cruelty of the trial, the hetero-suggestion of the women's examiners, and the perjuring of their witnesses, was more than they could endure, so in despair they *all* pleaded " guilty " as a quick termination to their sufferings. The whole six of them were burned.

Another account illustrating the manner in which people were implicated, and eventually hastened toward what came to be regarded as the inevitable end, is given in the old chronicles of Monstrelet. It states that at Arras, in the middle of the fifteenth century, there existed a coven of " certain persons, both men and women, who, under cover of night, by power of the Devil, repaired to some solitary spot amid the woods, where he appeared to them in human form, save that his visage was never perfectly visible." He was then said to read to the assembly a book of his ordinances, informing them how he would be obeyed and the punishment he would inflict for disobedience, distribute a little money, provide a plentiful meal, and conclude by a revel of general profligacy; after which each one of the party would be conveyed home in a mysterious manner.

On being accused of taking part in such acts of madness, several creditable persons of the town of Arras were seized and imprisoned along with some foolish women of little consequence. These were so horribly tortured that some of them—perhaps thinking of the old Bulgarian proverb : " Better an end in horror than horror without end "— *admitted as truth* all that they had been accused of ; and then, with contagious malice, they said they had seen and recognised in their nocturnal assemblies many persons of rank belonging to their own and other cities.

Several of those who had been informed against were thereupon arrested, thrown into prison and tortured ; after which those who

were poor were executed and inhumanly
burned, while the richer and more powerful
of the accused ransomed themselves by large
sums of money. Others there were, of a
truth, that suffered with marvellous patience
the torments inflicted on them, and would
confess nothing.

The foregoing are just a few examples of
witch-cases at random; comparatively, they
are representative of *minor* conflicts between
the judiciary or ecclesiastical courts and those
that were either daft enough to believe anything, or unfortunate enough to be victims
of malevolence and superstition. There were
other witch-trials and witch-huntings that
assumed the proportions of holocausts—
burning out whole communities.

In three months (in 1515) in the small
Bishopric of Bamberg 600 people were
burned; in Wurtzburg, 900; and in Geneva,
500; while in Toulouse, 400 were burned in
a year; and in Douay, 50. In the opening of
1586, the Archbishop of Trèves burned 118
women and 2 men who had all confessed under
torture to being witches, and therefore responsible by their spells and incantations
for the severe winter of 1585 and the late

spring of 1586. In 1597, Nicholaus Remingius, a judge of Lorraine, confessed to having condemned more than 900 in fifteen years. At Brescia, in Italy, in the year 1510, men and women were burned to the number of 140, and at Como during the same period 300 suffered the extreme penalty. The Inquisition (1254–1404) accounted for the great number of 30,000. And, as all know, Joan of Arc, the Maid of Orleans, was burned as a witch at Rouen in 1431—by the English !

As showing how even Continental stories of witchcraft, spells, and so on are not without a touch of humour, we quote the following :

In the eleventh century, Poppo, Archbishop of Trêves, sent a piece of his cloak to a nun with the request that she would make him a pair of slippers in which he might stand when saying mass. Now the nun had a dying love for Poppo, so when she made the slippers she bewitched them in the bargain. When the slippers were worn the spell began to work ; so the archbishop, to resist temptation and to deceive the devils working for his destruction, gave the slippers to one of his chief ecclesiastics, who before very long began to experience the same old feeling. Then *he* gave them away, and quietly they went from one to another of the whole of the clergy of Trèves Cathedral. The secret, however, becoming generally known, and the evidence being overwhelming, the fair offender was condemned to expulsion. The authorities, feeling that the discipline of the nunnery had become dangerously lax, gave the other nuns option of adopting a more strict rule, or of dispersion. They chose the latter, and were replaced by a body of monks.

Another : A demon story is related of St. Gregory. A nun once came to him with the information that while walking in the garden of the convent she had eaten a lettuce leaf without first marking the sign of the cross, and that immediately afterwards she felt herself possessed of a demon. St. Gregory thereupon exorcised the demon, and to such an extent that it called out upon him saying, " It wasn't my fault, I was only sitting on the leaf, and she ate me ! " Poor little devil !

CHAPTER VI

WEREWOLVES AND VAMPIRES

PROBABLY, the strangest of all strange things connected with witchcraft was the widespread belief that witches themselves could turn into werewolves either by their own free will or otherwise, and that a similar change of nature could be made to operate upon anybody else if the witches so desired. It was believed that the witches had only to put the spell of the evil eye upon someone, and that someone would fall into what was known as " wolf-fever," and that when the frenzy was at its height the stricken persons would discard all clothing and take to the woods. There they would live in holes or in trunks of trees, the finger- and toe-nails would be allowed to grow into claws, hair would cover the body, and wolflike habits be acquired.

That men have been able either by magic or natural gift to change themselves into ravening beasts has been one of the most prevalent and widespread ideas the world has ever known. Originating far back in barbaric life it has run like an hereditary taint through succeeding ages to within comparatively recent times. So much so indeed, that in many parts of the world where wolves abound it was forbidden for anyone to speak of them, "lest the wolves should hear and rend you."

It was not always into wolves, however, that the witches changed themselves; in India, it was tigers and leopards; in Africa, lions and hyenas; in Iceland, bears; and in England—as it is so long since wolves ran wild—the transformation was from witches to cats.

In a less enlightened age, when the sorcerer was thought capable of turning men into beasts by the aid of magic, the idea would have spread far and wide; and, supported by imagination and superstition, it is not surprising that it held such sway in the popular fancy. After all, the notion is quite consistent with the animistic theory of man's soul going out of his body and entering that of some animal, beast, or bird which in life he had taken kindly to. In mythology there are many references to such metamorphoses.

Hence the mythological term " lycanthropy " that has been given to it.

Then also it must be remembered, as Tylor says, that " the sorcerers who induced assemblies of credulous savages to believe in it were also the professional spiritualistic mediums or priests of the tribes, whose business it was to hold intercourse with the spirits of the dead, causing them to appear visibly, or by carrying on audible dialogues with them in dark and hollow places noted for giving a good echo and thereby create fear of such things in the minds and the hearts of the people "; for fear, as Shakespeare says, " sees more devils than vast hell can hold." Yet, notwithstanding all the arguments of theorists against the belief, those that have travelled in foreign parts where the werewolf belief is freely indulged in have some strange stories to tell. For instance, Pierce, in his *Life and Adventure*, relates that in Abyssinia a tribe of Budas are credited with the power of changing themselves into hyenas so frequently that the whole tribe are looked upon with execration. Pierce had a friend whose business took him among this particular people, and one day a servant of his—one of the tribe—came and asked for leave of absence, which was granted.

The servant departed, and in a few minutes the others called out, "Look! Look! He is turning himself into a hyena"; and, sure enough, some hundreds of yards away was the servant now turned into a hyena. This is all very strange, and the most remarkable thing about it is yet to be told. This tribe all wear a peculiarly shaped earring, and whenever a hyena is shot or trapped it is always found to have one of these rings of the exact pattern in its ear.

The inference, of course, is that the hyena before it became a hyena was one of the tribe of Budas.

Dalton, in his *Nota-Chagpore*, mentions how among the Ho of Singboom the wife of a man named Morn was killed by a tiger. The woman's husband, observing the occurrence, went in pursuit of the tiger till it entered a house in which there lived a man named Poosa. Morn with much courage followed even to the house, knocked at the door, and in reply to enquiries as to the business of his errand told them what had happened. They replied to the effect that they knew Poosa had the power of turning himself into a tiger at will. They then went in, bound him with ropes, and brought him out to Morn, who in revenge killed him. The authorities upon hearing of it caused enquiries to be made of the relatives concerning the strange business, and they learned that on a previous night he killed and devoured a goat, all the while that he was tearing it roaring like a tiger. On another night Poosa said he wanted to kill a bullock, but they would not allow him out of the house. In the morning there was only the remains of a bullock in the meadow. It had been killed by a tiger during the night.

While the preceding account may be taken as an example of willing compliance or voluntary metamorphosis, we have here one in which the werewolf or wereleopard had no control whatever over his actions, and simply did that for which fate had marked him down.

Two men of a certain tribe in Africa had disappeared, and rumour gave it out that they had been killed by a leopard. Traces of blood on the nephew of the tribe's chieftain led to a suspicion of his having killed them. He was sent for by the chieftain, and confessed to it ; and furthermore, he indicated where the mangled bodies of the two men were to be found. A search was made, and they were discovered in the forest, torn almost beyond description. Upon further questioning, the nephew explained that he couldn't help it; indeed, he bore them no ill, and so didn't want to kill them. He had been overlooked and had turned into a leopard against his own wish or desire, and while a leopard he simply did as leopards do. Upon returning to his own nature he was shocked at what he had done. The chief, although fond of his nephew, could not tolerate the fear of thinking that perhaps even he might fall a victim and be torn to pieces, so ordered that the nephew be burned to death.

Another remarkable feature in connection with lycanthropy was that so often when a werewolf was injured or wounded, someone else—the real person to whom the spirit in the werewolf belonged—was injured or wounded after the same manner; was this supposed to be accounted for by a duality of feeling and personality? The following will explain what is meant.

A man is out at night and meets a witch who endeavours to place a spell upon him. Suddenly the witch vanishes, and in her place stands a huge wolf.   The man having a scythe with him, thrusts it through the heart of the wolf.   When he arrives home he finds his own mother, whom he had never suspected of being a witch, dead, with a wound through the heart.

Another : A woodman cutting wood in a forest outside Strasbourg was attacked by three enormous cats, which after a fearful encounter he managed to beat off with a cudgel. Upon his return to town he was arrested on a charge of maltreating three well-known and respectable ladies of the place. He protested, declaring that he had seen no ladies since he left home in the morning, and showed his captors how scratched he was in consequence of his escapade with the three cats.   However, he was not believed ; and the representatives of law and order, to prove they were right and he was wrong, had the ladies examined by the court, whereupon it was declared they bore very real evidence of the chastisement complained of.

The counterpart to this last narrative is to be found in the story of the witches of Scotland, where at a Thurso witch-trial it was alleged by one of the witnesses that on many a night he had been tormented by witches, who in the shape of cats had gathered by moonlight outside his house and made most horrible noises, so that he could not sleep. On the previous night, when compelled to get up on account of their torments, he went into the garden, sword in hand, and laid about him in so terrific a manner as to cut off a leg from one not so nimble as the others in getting away. He added that on picking it up he was surprised to find it to be a human leg, and in the morning to his further amazement he had discovered the person to whom it really belonged. She was one of those accused of witchcraft. And his evidence was believed !

Of all the places of the earth the Danubian countries, perhaps, can boast of the greater number of werewolf stories.

In Hungary, the popular belief was that men usually turned into wolves by choice, but that women did so because of their sins ; so they at least couldn't help being werewolves. The man, however, before he can change his nature, has to adorn himself with a girdle of human skin ; and so long as the girdle is worn he remains a werewolf, and, what is of even greater importance, his old friends are not able to detect his werewolfism. If it should so happen that the woman cannot become a werewolf because she has no sins, then the difficulty can be overcome by the putting on of a wolfskin. This engenders a fierce disposition and a ravenous appetite. Her children mysteriously disappear, as also do those of her neighbours. And so the spell continues until she is caught and brought to the priest for treatment.

In Hungary as late as the year 1881 the wife of a gipsy fiddler was declared to have been a werewolf—having a particular fancy for sheep. It was also declared that so successfully did she follow her bent that she was able to provide her family with as much mutton as ever they needed, and in addition, to have been able to sell such a quantity as to provide her husband with enough capital to purchase an inn with. There probably would have been a lot more to tell of this had not the neighbouring peasants taken it upon themselves to murder the innkeeper. The priest was then called in, and he cured the woman by the sprinkling of holy water. However—and this is to the point—in the year 1900 there resided in the village of Tórésy at least two of the peasants who boasted of the fact that they had taken an active part in despatching the fiddling innkeeper.

At Besançon, in France, in the sixteenth century, three werewolves were trapped, and examined by the Inquisitor of the district of Dijon. They had been living in the woods apparently for some years, and had succeeded in spreading terror far and wide, so that all manner of extravagant stories were in circulation concerning them. And, of course, imagination entering into the repetition of them, the same stories magnified their number tremendously. Whole packs of wolves—wolves as big as horses—were declared to have been seen by all manner of people and on all manner of occasions. Still, these three were caught, and they were wild, demented creatures. At their trial they all confessed in a strange language hardly understandable how the Devil had given them wolves for wives, and that was the commencement of all the trouble. One admitted that he had killed a little boy and eaten him after having torn him to pieces, and the others confessed to having killed and eaten five children. The superstition of the period allowed the story to be acceptable, so the three were condemned and burned.

Although from the sixteenth century on-

wards the intellectuals of France did much to
discourage belief in such fantasms, the ideas
concerning werewolves have never got quite
clear of the peasants' mind. We have it on
the authority of Baring-Gould that only
about twenty years ago from now he found it
impossible when in France to get a guide to
conduct him after dark across a lonely wild
part of the Argonne said to be haunted by a
werewolf or *loup-garou*.

In the literature of the ages the references
to lycanthropy are many and varied and
are extremely interesting, inasmuch as they
give an insight into a particular phase of
belief that has by now almost disappeared.
It is evident also that besides its being possible
for men and women to change themselves
into wolves and other animals, it was no less
difficult for them to turn into foul and ominous birds (the pun is unintentional). The
following extract culled from the ancient writings of Apuleius shows this very distinctly :
" Pamphile divested herself of all her gar-
ments, and opening a certain cabinet took out
of it a number of boxes. From one of these
she selected a salve, and anointed herself
from head to foot ; and after much muttering,

she began to rock and wave herself to and fro. Presently a soft down covered her limbs, and a pair of wings sprang from her shoulders ; her nose became a beak ; her nails talons. Pamphile was now in form a complete owl. Then, uttering a low shriek, she began to jump from the floor, and after a brief while flew out of the window and vanished."

By way of showing how far-flung and how long-lived these old ideas are, we are reminded by Horace Walpole in his *Reminiscences* how His August Majesty King George I, when in a tender mood, promised one of his mistresses, the Duchess of Kendal, that if he were to die before her, and if it were possible, he would return to her occasionally just to pass the compliments of the season and so on. Now the king did die first, and of course the duchess fully expected him to keep his promise. So when a distracted raven flew in at one of her windows at Isleworth, she could not help but think and believe it to be anything else than the soul of the king come to her in the shape of a bird. And she treated it accordingly.

The werewolves were no seven days' wonder ; they were the terror of a thousand years— perhaps longer. No wonder the recollection of them was so difficult to eradicate ; the belief had taken too firm an anchorage.

To-day, in folk-story and in fairy-tale, we yet have reminders of them, although so veiled are they with the excrescence of the centuries that they are hardly discernible. To mention a few, there is Grimm's story of *The Wolf and the Seven Kids* ; there is the narrative of Llewellyn, *Gelert and the Wolf*, and the familiar *Red Riding Hood* ; and last but not least there is the historical story of Romulus, the founder of Rome, being suckled by a wolf when as an infant he was cast into the Tiber and left high and dry by the receding flood.

Closely allied to the werewolves were the vampires, and extraordinary as it may seem that anyone could have believed in the story of the former, more extraordinary still was it that anyone could be found to put their faith in the existence of the latter. Yet at one time it was a generally accepted possibility that any dead body having become bewitched would become a vampire ; or, for that matter, anyone who had been cursed by their parents, or had been excommunicated by the Church, was thought to be qualified. Witches were supposed to turn into vampires after they were buried, as also was the corpse of anyone else which before burial had been jumped over by a cat [1] or flown over by a bird.

The term " vampire " is of Slavonic origin, and means a bloodsucking ghost. This ghost was supposed to leave the grave in which it was buried at night-time, and suck the blood from the necks of the living, when it would return once more to the grave. In shape and form it was simply a head with entrails attached.

The superstition was, and still is, prevalent in Eastern Europe. It was especially popular at that period when prosecution and punishment for alleged witchcraft in Western Europe was drawing to an end—the beginning of the eighteenth century. The word itself had

---

[1] In Scotland apparently there was a like idea, for Pennant, in his *Tour of Scotland*, tells us that on the death of a highlander it was customary to place the body on a board and to cover it with a linen wrapper, after which the friends would place upon the breast a wooden platter containing a small quantity of salt and earth—the earth being the emblem of the corruptible body, while the salt represented the immortal spirit. Watch would then be kept to see that no dog or cat passed over the body. So ominous was it reckoned that if either did, it would be killed without mercy.

never, so far as is known, been used in England until 1734.

Another odd idea attached to the belief was that the souls of those qualified for vampirism could come from the grave—unless it had a very heavy gravestone [1]—assume the shape of a straw or a piece of fluff, and then could fall on the neck of a sleeper and suck away the life-blood. [2] If a person died from having been bitten by a vampire, then that person would probably also become one. But this did not happen to all who were bitten, neither did it occur all at once, for the bitten person had to go through varied stages of development.

First of all the person bitten would fall into a kind of death-trance simulating death, and in this condition would be buried. Until the body was buried it was impossible for it to turn vampire, but as bodies could not be kept

[1] Were gravestones first used to keep the ghost in? One wonders.

[2] In the zoological kingdom there are bloodsucking bats (S. America) known as vampires. These bats have very sharp teeth with which they make a punctured wound in the neck of horses, cattle, and other animals (and human beings) when asleep. From the punctured wound they gorge themselves with blood, swelling visibly as progress is made.

above ground indefinitely, one never knew what was likely to happen.

In the course of time these vampires became so plentiful and such a nuisance that the authorities were compelled to take proceedings against them. As the vampires were mere ghosts they could not, of course, be apprehended, so the next best thing to do was to visit the graveyards, find out where the bodies belonging to the vampires rested, and then stake them to the earth [1] or fire a pistol at their head—presumably to kill the spirit.

A vampire's body was detected by its deportment and appearance in the coffin. If it had rosy cheeks and blood on its lips, and had its limbs drawn up, then it *was* a vampire, or it may be that since it was buried its finger-nails had lengthened and it had grown a beaver. All these, and more, were taken as definite proofs.

One or two of the best known narratives concerning vampires will now be given, and

[1] In England until the time of George IV it was the common practice to bury suicides at cross roads, with a stake driven through the chest. If the stake did not keep the ghost in, then the fact of its coming to the surface at the cross roads—presuming it wanted to come to the surface—would fill it with dismay. It would not know which way to go, and would return.

as nearly all the narratives are remarkably similar in make-up these few may pass as types. They have been shorn, however, of some of their superfluously horrible detail.

Near Belgrade, so the story goes—and this is a chestnut with the tellers of ghost stories— there was a young man named Arnod who had returned from Cossova, where, he declared, the people were dying of fright on account of their friends being bitten by a vampire. He himself had not been bitten ; but he had been in the vampire's presence, and the vampire had made him understand that he was soon to die and become a vampire also.[1] Sure enough, a few days afterwards he fell into a death-trance and was buried.

Three weeks afterwards a girl named Nina, who had known him, together with some neighbours, complained that a vampire was haunting them with unwelcome attention, and that four people had been bitten in the neck and had died in consequence.

Such a serious state of things could not be allowed to continue ; so the authorities, on a grey morning a day or two afterwards, made up a nondescript party consisting of a sexton,

---

[1] In cases of this kind the eating of earth from the vampire's grave was considered the only safe cure.

two surgeons, armed with spades, pickaxes, and ropes, together with one drummer boy from the army carrying a lantern and a box of surgical instruments, and they wended their way to the churchyard where Arnod, the vampire, lay buried.

Their intention was to find out for certain whether he *was* a vampire or not. If he proved himself to be one, then he would be treated as all vampires were treated.

They reached the cemetery, found the grave they were in search of, and began to dig with a right good will. Presently, the pickaxe struck the coffin lid and pulled it off, and *there* was Arnod lying on his side " *asleep*."

The sexton pulled him over, gazed at him, and then in a voice of triumph cried out, " What ! Your mouth not wiped since last night's escapade ! "—and other things eminently suitable to the occasion, but which are of no concern to us. At this the spectators shuddered ; the boy dropped the lantern and the instruments into the grave, and promptly fell in after them.

When the boy, the lantern, and the instruments had been picked up, sorted out and put together again, further attention was paid **to Arnod.**

As was expected, he proved himself a true vampire, for " his face did have a complexion upon it " and he " did appear as though he had not been dead a day." So without any further ado he was spiked, and as this was being done " the corpse groaned." The body was then taken up, burned as if it were a witch, and the ashes scattered to the wind.

Other coffins in the same cemetery being opened, four of them upon examination were found to contain vampires, so a similar treatment was meted out to them. Such decisive measures as these, however, failed to extinguish the evil which was believed to be blighting the village, so a more severe reprisal was inaugurated.

The authorities had *all* the graves opened, every body was anatomised, and where it was thought advisable the bodies were treated as Arnod's had been.

These happenings, as improbable as they may appear to have been, are recorded as having taken place at Mednegna, near Belgrade, in 1832. The report is signed by three regimental surgeons, and countersigned by a lieutenant-colonel and a sub-lieutenant. It was published in the newspapers of the day, with reservation, and must have been told thousands of times since with modification.

Another account concerns the district of Kring, where a man died and became a vampire. As he became a nuisance also, and the cause of many deaths, it was decided to give *him* the usual treatment. Although he had been dead some days, it was discovered upon opening his coffin that his face had not only a fresh appearance, but that " his lips smiled." He even opened his mouth, so it is asserted, as if to take in air. On this occasion a priest was sent for, who upon arrival held a crucifix before the half-opened eyes, crying out at the same time in a loud voice—" See, this is Jesus Christ who died for you and redeemed your soul from hell."

As the voice with its message acted upon the dead man's hearing, he began to weep; and the authorities believing this and other strange happenings to be proof that he was a vampire, dismissed the priest, and promptly hacked off his head. As the head rolled away from the body there came from it—so it is declared—" a terrible screech which struck dumb terror into the souls of those living witnesses from whose company it had departed." Enough !

Many other narratives of a similar character could be given—but are they worth telling? Vampires are alleged to have made themselves troublesome, but the accounts are entirely lacking in trustworthy testimony sufficient in quantity to give them the stamp of credence. In fact, most of the evidence is even more trivial than that connected with the local Saturday night ghost stories of a hundred or so years ago. The stories even have about them an atmosphere of horrible bravado and concoction of detail suggestive of dementia in its most acute form. Thank goodness that the witches of England only turned into cats, and not into bloodsucking ghouls!

But after all, the belief as to the existence of vampires was undoubtedly a very firm one. How came it to be such? Can an acceptable explanation be found?

While neither expecting nor hoping to solve the riddle, we can at least, by a careful examination of what meagre facts there are, come to some conclusions that will give to some extent what might have been a reason for the belief.

There can be no doubt but that when those coffins were opened there was distinct evidence that the body in many instances was not in such a reposeful state as it should have been had nothing untoward happened. In many cases it is quite likely that the inmates were the victims of premature burial, and that, awakening to life after they had been buried, they had made frantic efforts towards freedom. This in some measure would account for them being found—when coffins were opened—with their knees drawn up, lying on their side, and so on.

This premature burying was frightfully prevalent up to a few years ago. Dr. Fontanelli (1860) recorded forty-six cases of premature burial, and claimed to have had actual knowledge of six interments of living persons in eight months in Paris alone. Another authority, Professor Carri, asserted that he knew of forty-six cases during his professional career, and among these no fewer than twenty-one returned to life at the time they were about to be buried. Nine came to life on account of the affectionate attention bestowed on them by their relatives at funeral time. Four woke up on account of their coffins being carelessly dropped, and three because their shroud pins penetrated their flesh. Seven others were

prevented a premature burial through unusual delay in interment.

That was in France; in England, fortunately,
the danger of being buried alive is practically
inconsiderable, though one may often come
across little items of intelligence, such as
codicils in wills, stipulating that a sum of £20
or so is set on one side for the family physician
on condition that he assures himself that the
testator or testatrix is really and truly dead
before burial takes place.[1]

In America, where presumably the fear of
premature burial is feared and expected more
than in some other parts of the world, a
society was founded in the year 1900 for the
Prevention of Premature Burial[2]; and no
wonder, as will be seen in a moment.

[1] This probably was but a perpetuation of the old
custom, with modification, of placing a small Greek
coin, or *obolus*, in the mouth of a corpse before interment as payment to Charon for " ferrying the soul."
Charon, in mythology, was the son of Erebus, a deity
of Hades ; it was in his power to conduct the souls of
the dead across the river Styx to the judgment seat.
Styx was the principal river of the lower regions which
it encompassed seven times and *had* to be crossed by
the shades of the departed before they could enter
therein.

[2] A society was also formed in London for the same
purpose in 1895.

Seventy-five years earlier coffins in New York presented for burial were kept for eight days open at the head and so arranged that the least movement inside would cause a bell to ring. Out of twelve hundred tested in this manner, six returned to life—one in every two hundred.

With regard to the condition of the finger-nails and beard being taken as evidence, or even as proof, of the existence of life after burial, there has been some controversy as to whether or not these continue to grow even after a person *is* dead. On referring to the works of a renowned toxicologist, the opinion is there expressed that both hair and nail may grow for a time after death; and that this has been proved by careful observations.

Dr. Bicet, in the *French Dictionary of Medical Science*, says : " Molecular life and fecundity of the epidermis and therefore of the hair follicles for a time after death is what theory would lead us to expect, and observations are ample in proof."

In corroboration of the previous idea we have had it on the authority of a doctor of medicine of Iowa that at an exhumation attended by him where the body had been buried four years, it was found that the coffin had given way at the joists and that the hair had protruded through the opening. He also had evidence, he said, to show that deceased was shaved before burial, nevertheless his hair measured eighteen inches, while beard and whiskers had grown to eight inches!

This last episode occurred a generation or so ago, and so much was written about it and so notorious did the accounts of it become that at last the sting of it all was taken away by ridicule and jest. Popular songs and street ballads by the score were ascribed to it, and as these lines are being penned there comes to mind the sound of the street boys shouting:

Still his whiskers grew. Still his whiskers grew.
They hammered him down, they nailed him down,
They lathered and shaved the top of his grave,
But still his whiskers grew!

We will leave it at that.

CHAPTER VII

BLOOD AND FIRE IN ENGLAND

THE two previous chapters have been inserted that readers might all the more easily be able to appreciate the progress of witchcraft in England by means of comparison with that on the Continent. We will now return to the conditions of social life in England at that period when witchcraft trials were most prevalent.

The statute of Henry VIII (1541) forbidding either the belief in, or the practice of "witchcraft" and declaring it a felony was repealed by Elizabeth some years later; but was followed by another, and from this time onward for many years there was a continuous run of trials, exposures in the pillory, and executions all over the land. Nor is it to be wondered at, for in Archbishop Cranmer's articles on Visitation (1549) it is required that "you shall enquire whether you know of any that use charms, sorcery, soothsayings, enchantments, or any like craft invented by the Devil." The consequence was that everyone became inquisitive regarding their neighbour.

Then, in 1558, Bishop Jewel thought it advisable to remind the same Queen that " within the last few years the witches and sorcerers have increased marvellously." The sequel to this was the passing of another Act in 1562, in which it was ordained that " *if any person is wasted or injured by witchcraft, the offenders shall suffer a year's imprisonment and be pilloried four times, and that on the second offence the death penalty shall be pronounced.*"

This Jewel of a bishop had recently returned from exile on the Continent, whence he had fled on account of Queen Mary's persecution, so that he became fully acquainted with the Continental method for the extirpation of witches, and may, possibly, have used his power to retaliate upon the Catholics, for whom, it may be believed, he had no particular affection. However, he was afterwards made Bishop of Salisbury. Writing to a friend soon after his return to England, he said : " We found in all places relics of saints, nails with which the infatuated people dreamed that Christ had been pierced, and I know not what small fragments of the sacred cross." Then he significantly added : " The number of witches and sorceresses have everywhere become enormous." Couple with the last sentence of the Bishop's letter the popular belief of the period—and indeed for two hundred years afterwards—that witchcraft was spread in England by roving Jesuit priests, and, remembering the statute imposing the death penalty, we may easily imagine the application of the law to the belief to have proved an effective "short way" with Catholics.

Hunting down the witches, bringing about a conviction, and carrying out the sentence would indeed be no very difficult operation, for there was money in it, and besides, the land then literally bristled with gibbets and gallows. In most part they were the legacy left by a law passed at the beginning of the thirteenth century which forbade every male over the age of fifteen to harbour malefactors, robbers, thieves, and outlaws, and called upon them, one and all, to chase and give evidence against all whom they knew to be, or suspected of being, such.

As the majority of the people in those poor old days were either malefactors, robbers, thieves, or outlaws, there was a corresponding need for gallows and such-like constructions, and, as timber was then very plentiful and executioners fairly well paid for their despatch work, the law of supply and demand worked exceedingly well.

Apparently, anybody that was anybody at all had power to set up a gibbet. For instance, the Abbot of Westminster erected as many as sixteen in Middlesex alone. As an ecclesiastic he *gave sanctuary* to the thieves ; and then as LORD of the manor he handed them over to his bailiff to be hanged !

The great Tyburn gallows that stood near where the Marble Arch now stands at Hyde Park, London, and on which not a few men and women were executed as witches, was a triangular arrangement of three uprights with beams across from corner to corner—and on busy occasions would have hanging from *each* beam as many as eight—twenty-four at once ! As the gallows was in constant use, it was customary to take off the bodies when lifeless, and then either bury them near by or re-hang them on the gibbets erected close at hand, where they would continue to hang until they fell to pieces—that is, if they had not suffered the indignity of being quartered.

In very old prints the gallows at Tyburn are referred to as "THE ELMS," and in this connection it is of interest to call to mind that in the long past the elm was the Norman tree of justice : under its branches the judges sat in judgment. The probability is that the Tyburn gallows were of Norman origin.

From the time when "Adam delved and Eve span" the tree has played not an unimportant part in human aspirations. To the Druids the oak was sacred and in the days of the oldest of the Oracles the oak was credited with oracular powers. At the Oracle of Lesbos there grew a laurel, the leaves of which upon being eaten by the priestess would instil wisdom and power. And so we might go on, were this a treatise on arboriculture and not witches.

To return to the gallows : The minimum sum stolen that qualified a thief for hanging seems to have been the proverbial fourpence. Earlier, in Athelstan's time, it was twelvepence, so you see, we got better—or worse—as we got older. In 1130, when Henry I founded a priory, he made over with it " all rights, including a *free* gallows for hanging thieves on."

As bad as a gallows-hanging undoubtedly was, as a corrector of moral and political inexactitudes, it was evidently thought to be not bad enough for witches, for in 1222 Stephen Langstan, Archbyshoppe of Cantaburie, presided over a court where an old woman and a young man were accused of witchcraft, and " for such crime " were " adjudged to be closed up between two walls of stone that they might end their lives miserably "—that is, they were taken whilst alive and plastered *into* a wall !

Another horrible form of punishment was that of " PRESSING." The procedure was to place the victim flat upon the floor with legs and arms outstretched in the form of an X and fastened to iron rings. A sharp stone as big as a fist would be pushed under the small of the back, and then a wide board or door would be placed on the body ; upon this would be loaded iron weights and lumps of stone to the amount of several hundredweight.

Then later, in Henry VIII's time (1530), a Richard Roose was charged for an attempt to poison by means of witchcraft the Reverend Father in God, John, Byshoppe of Rochester, at old Lambeth Palace. As the gallows was not terrible enough punishment —although it carried with it the punishment of the hanged man having his bowels torn out by the executioner and burned *before* he was dead, and then of his body being " quartered "—a special Act was passed whereby it was decreed that " the said Richard Roose shall therefore be *boiled* to death *without having Benefit of Clergy*." Nor was this the only instance of horrible horridness, for Stow records how in 1542 Margaret Davy, a maid-servant, was *boiled* to death at Smithfield. This was called " Capital Punishment," and verily it was—with an emphasis on the CAPITAL.

The meaning of the term "benefit of clergy," although now obsolete and without any real meaning in this century of grace, was, at the time of which we are thinking, of some importance. By a statute of Edward III, a clerk in Holy Orders, if arrested for a misdemeanour under the law, or even on a charge of murder, if it was a first offence, would be able to claim the privilege, or right, to the benefit, which was that he be not sent to the gallows right away, but that he should be given another chance.

So that the culprit would not get the benefit

a second time, he was carefully branded on the back with a hot iron—an " M " for a murderer or an " F " for having committed a felony.

In time the benefit was made to extend to others besides clerks in Holy Orders, so that anyone of education and learning finding themselves in awkward situations could also claim its privileges. Applicants for the benefit, to show that they were learned, had to read one of the Psalms, printed in Latin. It was commonly spoken of as " the neck psalm."

Had it not been for this clause in the statute, English literature would have lost its Rare Ben Jonson, for on occasion of a brawl similar to that in which Marlowe was killed he had slain in Hoxton Fields an actor, of the Rose, Bankside. Instead of being hanged, he was branded with an " M " and sent to prison for a short period. Afterwards, soliloquising on the event, he wrote :

" Playwright, convicted of public wrong to men,
    Takes private beatings and begins again."

During the Elizabethan period a change seems to have come over the old witchcrafts. They no longer—except on rare occasions—continued to meet at cross-roads, or to be performances of obscene rites at Witches' Sabbaths ; but consisted more or less in soothsayings, divinations, conjurations and the casting of spells for religious and political purposes, or for the supposed purpose of injury to the person, damage to crops, and the abortion of cattle—all of which possibilities were explicitly believed in.

Also, the charges against witches which had been left almost entirely to ecclesiastical jurisdiction, now passed definitely to the State. The statute of Elizabeth, including as it did power of conviction against persons for all manner of legerdemain, had been made to apply to almost every form of thought and action if it came under suspect on account of its unorthodoxy. Moreover, as the period of which we are writing was the dawn of England's intellectual awakening, it came about, through the agitated ignorance of the masses, that all which could not be accounted for off-hand in the ordinary way, or by the application of recently acquired but imperfect knowledge, or could not be understood on account of its novelty, was at once put down to magic, necromancy, witch-spells, or the Devil.

To such an extent did the bias of public

opinion lean in its apportioning of the blame for bad crops, storms, pestilence, and so on, against the witches, that we find in the general literature of the day many a pithy sentence which by their repetition go to show that the idea must have been common to the period. For instance, Thomas Gale, writing in 1562, says : " I did see in two hospitals in London known as St. Thomas' and St. Bartholomew's, to the number of three hundred and odd poor people that were diseased, all of whom were brought to this mischief by witches, and I, with certain others, diligently examined these people as to how they came by their grievous hurts, and who their chirurgeons were that looked unto them, and they confessed that they were either witches which did promise charms to make them whole, or else some women which would make them whole with herbs and such-like things. But what manner of cures they did I tell you—*such cures as maketh the Devil in Hell to dance for joy to see the poor members of Jesus Christ so miserably tormented* " !

Another extraordinary thing about the dismal business was, that men and women of noble birth and attainment should have embraced it, for their own aggrandisement or for some religio-political motive ; and so become so evidently self-condemned as to have no real defence when the charge of guilt happened to be brought against them.

Thus we find Sir Anthony Fortescue, a second cousin of Queen Elizabeth, "consorting with witches" for the purpose of causing the queen's death and placing Mary, Queen of Scots, on the throne in her stead. The charge involved other men of rank, such as the Spanish and French ambassadors as well as two nephews of Cole, Archbishop of Canterbury, who, by the way, had been Queen Mary's supreme adviser when her persecution of Protestants was most severe.

There is an old saying that "every crisis finds a hero," and in connection with witchcraft there is probably no greater hero than Reginald Scot,[1] an Oxford scholar and country gentleman resident in Kent, who in the year 1584 issued his remarkably outspoken work

[1] Reginald Scot (c. 1538–99), a younger son of Sir John Scot of Scotshall in Kent. He published in 1574 *The Hoppe Garden* (which went through three editions in four years) and is credited with the introduction of hop-growing into England.

entitled *The Discoverie of Witchcraft*.[1] His book was an exposure of the childish absurdities which formed the basis of the witchcraft craze, a bold appeal to popular reason, and a brave attempt at persuading the Crown as well as the populace against too severe a condemnation of people who by petulance or spite were dubbed "witches." As events proved, Reginald Scot, like other reformers, lived a hundred or so years before his time.

That the book perturbed the peace of mind of a good many people there can be little doubt, and not least among them was James, King of Scotland and heir-presumptive to the English throne. Having some ideas of his own on the subject of witchcraft, and deeming Scot's book obnoxious, he caused all copies of it to be gathered together and

[1] The contents page of the first edition is as follows. It is of some interest when read in comparison with that of the third: "The Discovery of Witchcraft, wherein the Lewde dealing of Witches and Witchmongers is notablie detected, the knaverie of Conjurers, the impietie of Inchantments, the follie of Soothsayers, the impietie of Atheists, the Vanitie of Dreamers and the beggarley art of Dreaming, the abomination of Idolatrie, the horrible art of Poisoning, the virtue and power of Natural Magick, Legerdemaine and Juggling, etc., etc. Hereunto is added a treatise upon the nature and substance of Spirits and Devils."

burned by the public hangman—but James was just a little too late ; the book had already done its good work.

The clearing away of the book of course cleared the way for another on the same subject, and who, to be sure, could supply it so well as James himself ? So, in a business-like manner, in 1597 he wrote down that peculiar collection of ideas known as *King James' Booke Against Witchcraft and Dæmonologie*, and had it published by Royal command.

That the king tilted against Reginald Scot there can be little doubt, for he made it quite clear—in kingly style—that he " wrote against the damnable opinions of Scot, who is not ashamed in public print to deny there can be such a thing as a witch."

Sixty years afterwards, when the king's book, like the king himself, was a back number, there appeared, phœnix-like, during the Puritan ascendancy, a second edition of Scot's *Discoverie* which James had suppressed and supplanted, and a revised third [1]

---

[1] " The Discovery of Witchcraft : proving that the Compacts and Contracts of Witches with Devils and all Infernal Spirits or Familiars are but Erroneous Novelties and Imaginary Conceptions, . . . their Power . . . in

edition was published in 1665. Occasionally, rare copies are to be found in the auctioneer's catalogues. In 1916 a copy was bought in this manner in London for £36 and in 1925 another for £85. Both books—Scot's and King James's—may be seen at the British Museum.

The king's ideas of witchcraft and demonology as expressed by him in his book without doubt kept alive and fostered in the imagination of the people the mysteries of the craft. He may have intended otherwise, and his book may have been issued for the express purpose of demolishing the whole fabric of witch belief and imposture; but it missed fire. It was *too* strong.

His animosity against witches and their evil practices was in all probability inherent. After a gloomy childhood, he signalised his

Killing, Tormenting, Consuming, or Curing the bodies of Men . . . or Animals, by Charms, Philtres, Periapts, Pentacles, Curses, and Conjurations, wherein likewise the Unchristian Practices and Inhuman Dealings of Searchers and Witch-tryers upon Aged, Melancholly, and Superstitious people, in extorting Confessions by Terrors and Tortures, . . . Knavery of Juglers, Conjurers, Charmers, Soothsayers, Figure-Casters, Dreamers, Alchymists and Philterers, with many other things, . . . whereunto is added an excellent Discourse of the Nature and Substance of Devils and Spirits."

accession to the English throne by a holy and terrific raid upon the agents of his mighty antagonist, the Devil. And the weapon he most relied upon was his own statute.

The statute repealed that of Elizabeth, and before becoming law was approved of by twelve bishops and six earls. It stipulated that "*any one using, practising, or exercising any innovation of any evil or wicked spirit, or consulting or employing any evil or wicked spirit to or for any purpose whatsoever, shall be deemed as offenders, and such offenders being duly and lawfully convicted shall suffer death. Moreover, if any person or persons shall use, practise, or exercise any innovation or conjuration of any evil and wicked spirit, or shall consult, covenant with, entertain, employ, feed, or reward any evil and wicked spirit to or for any intent or purpose, or take up any dead man, woman or child out of his, her, or their grave or any other place where the dead body resteth, or the skin, bone, or any part of any dead person to be employed or used in any manner of witchcraft, sorcerie, charm, or enchantment, or shall use, practise, or exercise any witchcraft, enchantment, charm, or sorcerie whereby any person shall be killed, destroyed, wasted, consumed, pined, or lamed in his or her body or any part*

*thereof, every such offender is a felon without
benefit of clergy."*

Previously, the law imposed the death
penalty only where *injury* by means of witchcraft had been proven; this new Act of James
made the mere belief in, or consulting with,
evil spirits subject to the same penalty.

James I and his advisers were out to attack
witchcraft not so much through their hatred
of the immorality of it, or for the protection
of the credulous from impostors, but rather
from their fear of the Devil and their suspicion towards all secret societies. If, as
was popularly believed, the king was God's
anointed, and the witches were the Devil's
servants, there was bound to be war to the
death between them. Enemies under the
guise of witches made attempts on the king's
life, and he retaliated through his witch-
hunters. The witches had formed a secret
organisation, they had defied their king and
his laws; they had made attempts on the
life of His Most Gracious Majesty, therefore
their institutions were treasonable and were
proceeded against accordingly—" without
benefit of clergy."

The king's zeal, perhaps, is not to be
wondered at, for he had been told by a devil,

speaking through a witch, that he was a man of God, and that the demons could have no power over him. In addition, he was well versed in all the traditional lore of his time, and so proved himself a bold, adventurous antagonist towards those that were desirous of casting their spells over him.

So little did he fear their influence that on consecutive days he would attend in person the trials and examinations. Small wonder was it that the many phases of grotesque horror which the confessions disclosed did put him into " a wonderful admiration."

On one occasion at a witch - trial, the accused—a deluded woman—confessed that she and another were in the habit of dancing a reel before the Devil in the kirk of Berwick. This amused the king so much that he there and then said he would like to be a witness to a repetition of the infernal performance. So off he went, with his varlets at his heels, in procession, at night-time, to the kirk-yard, and " did there observe the devil who upon the like trumpe did play the said dance before the king's Majestie. And the king in respect of the strangeness of these matters, did take great delight in being present."—Hoch!

That James could play the rascal's part

as well as that of the buffoon there can be little doubt, as the following incident illustrates. A stubborn prisoner—a barber-surgeon—refused to confess the guilt upon which he was charged, and, as the chronicler gives it, appeared to be " very solitairye." Whereupon the Majesty " perceiving the stubborn wilfulnesse " ordered that " his nayles upon his fingers should be riven and pulled with tunkas (a pincer-like instrument of torture) and that under every nayle there should be thrust two needles up even unto their heads. At all which torments, notwithstanding, the doctor never shrunke anie whitt, neither would he then confess it the sooner for all the tortures inflicted upon him. Then was he by commandment conveyed to the torment of THE BOOT (a crushing instrument), where he continued for a long time, and abode so many blows in them that his legs were crushed and beaten together as small as might be, and the bones and flesh so bruised that the blood and marrow spouted forth in great abundance, whereby they were made unserviceable for ever afterwards."

Notwithstanding James's efforts to suppress the witches, we find that in the reign of Charles I they were as numerous as ever, for in 1640 the General Assembly passed an Act calling upon all ministers " to take particular note of witches and charmers," and advising them that " the Commissioners should recommend to the supreme judicature *the unsparing application* of the laws against them."

This was supplemented three years afterwards by the granting of power to " *any understanding gentlemen or magistrates to apprehend, try, and execute justice against witches and charmers*." Then, a little later, as the Puritans gained strength, further powers were granted. The sequel was a tremendous increase in the number of charges and convictions, so much so that during the period of the Long Parliament there were, it is estimated, no fewer than three thousand persons in England alone that came under the capital charge and were either tortured, burned, or hanged.

In Scotland the suspects fared no better, for at a single circuit court held in 1659 as many as seventeen persons were charged, and the whole of them paid the extreme penalty.

During the whole of the seventeenth century the number of witch charges per year fluctuated according to the fervour of contending political and religious parties.

CHAPTER VIII

DEMONS AND MASCOTS

DEMONOLOGY, possession, witchcraft, and the black art belong one to the other, as darkness belongs to night. So resourceful at all times has been the imagination with regard to belief in the power of malignant spirits, that hardly any people or race has been exempt from it. Indeed, the whole religion of the heathen world rested upon the basis of demonism ; and when heathenism gave place to Christianity it bequeathed to it for eternal perpetuation many of its own mysterious beliefs and fears, which, with a striking fidelity, have continued their baneful influence through succeeding ages.

" There are few things so indestructible as a superstitious belief when once it has become fairly implanted in human credulity," says H. C. Lea in his *History of the Inquisition*, and never were truer words spoken. "It passes from one race to another and is handed down through countless generations ; it adapts itself successively to every form of religious faith ; persecution may stifle its outward manifestation, but it continues to be cherished in secret, perhaps the more earnestly because it is unlawful. Religion may succeed religion, but the change only multiplies the methods by which man seeks to supplement his impotence by obtaining control over supernatural powers. The sacred rites of the superseded faith become the forbidden magic of its successor and its gods become evil spirits.''

Just as the pagans of old saw in, through, and behind every happening the working of a god, satyr, genie, or demon, so the Fathers of the early Christian Church, with their doctrinal belief in supernatural powers, saw something similar. Small wonder, therefore, that there arose a philosophy of errors and heresies, which, being caught hold of, were adopted and transformed into all manner of weird conceptions by the intellectuals of their time, and which in turn showed themselves in an aggravated form in the superstitions and beliefs of the unlettered masses of the ignorant underworld.

The latter, being unable to read or write, and being simple withal, could comprehend only those parts of worship which they could associate with mere form, and then there evolved a whole system of symbol and ritual. The principle of evil became represented by hideous forms which haunted the mind by day and tormented the sleeper by night. And dreams would add to the confusion.

So every age has witnessed some form of superstitious belief in omens, oracles, necromancies, ghosts, spirits, goblins, fairies, and devils, together with a whole crowd of other creations too numerous to mention ; and these beliefs were never so apparent as at times of national misfortune or religious fervour.

A striking example of this symbolism just remarked upon is to be seen in the old Church of St. Peter, Chaldon, Surrey, in the form of panel pictures painted on the wall at a period when the folk for whom they were intended, being unable to read, could only comprehend the teaching of the times in which they lived by means of pictures. The paintings, though executed about the year 1200, were only discovered in 1870 when the church was undergoing some renovation. One part of the picture represents a cheating tradesman on a bridge of spikes, another a usurer with his money-bags around him in the flames. A dog-demon bites the feet of wicked dancers, and in the centre of the picture there is a ladder up which souls are climbing to Paradise. Some reach the top where Christ stands, others that fall off are boiled by demons in a seething cauldron, and so on.

The heyday of witchcraft practice and witch-trials in Europe synchronised with the Inquisition and the Reformation, and perhaps it is not to be wondered at, for the people of the period believed implicitly in the possibility and the reality of compacts with the Devil just to the extent of their belief in the dogma of the personality of the Devil himself.

The Inquisition and the Reformation confirmed, amongst other beliefs, the whole doctrine of the belief in Satan's *visible* agency on earth, together with the grotesque conception of his horrible dealings with the ill-starred children of men.

Demons, fiends, and spectres known as Succubi and Incubi lurked, it was supposed, in every dark hole and corner, and were thought to be prodigal in the amount of attention they gave to those who were willing enough to believe in their existence and to do their will. Satan himself was at warfare with

Heaven, and his main effort was to seduce human souls from their divine allegiance, consequently he was ever eager to tempt them with that which would seem most likely to suit his purpose.

To these incubi and succubi many strange and horrible powers were attributed, and however much in our enlightened age we may feel disposed to reject the possibility of the human mind ever having put faith in such tosh, it is nevertheless an accepted fact that there were a good many people at one time who most really and truly believed in both these demons, and furthermore, were willing and anxious to be participants in their unholy rites.[1]

If the reader is anything of a folklorist he will remember the once popular fallacy that many an old and noble family had its origin from such an alliance ; for instance, Robert of Normandy, known as " le Diable," is mentioned by old writers on demonology as the offspring of such ; as also was Merlin, the old enchanter.

[1] The Incubus was a lascivious demon appearing to women at night, and the Succubus a somewhat similar demon possessed of the power of assuming the form of a woman.

As we have said, the idea was at one time pretty world-wide, and was persisted in to comparatively modern times. Tylor in his work on *Primitive Culture*, written as late as in 1873, says, " Concerning the incubi and succubi, those male and female nocturnal demons which consort lasciviously with men and women, this is the doctrine: In the Islands of the West Indies they are the ghosts of the dead, vanishing when clutched at. In New Zealand ancestral deities form attachments with females, paying them repeated visits. In the Samoan Islands such intercourse with inferior gods was believed to have caused many supernatural conceptions. And in the Hindu Tantra formal rites are specified which enable a man to obtain a companion-nymph by worshipping at night in any burial-place."

St. Augustine in the sixth century stated the popular notions of his day regarding these things in England, but was careful not to commit himself to a belief in them. Later on, however, the theologians were less cautious and grave argumentation on nocturnal intercourse with incubi and succubi was carried on till at the height of mediæval civilisation it was accepted in full belief by ecclesiastics and lawyers ; scores of women being burned at the stake for having confessed to participation in the practice.[1]

It is more than probable, however, that in witchcraft days the part of the incubus was played by the chief of the witches' coven, in disguise—the witches being at too great a disadvantage in the dark to distinguish the difference during the ecstasy of their unholy joy.

By way of illustrating further how familiar these things were in a past age, the following narrative, told quite casually by Erasmus among his satires, is of interest.[2]

A man, with his wife and daughter, had been practising magic. He had at some time or other purchased for a small price the adorable body of Christ, which, for the want of a more suitable place, he kept under his bed. One night he brought the mystery out of the straw. The girl, a virgin, pointed at it

[1] On the Continent this sexual element—Concubitus dæmonum—first came into prominence in 1286. The Inquisition took cognisance of the first case of its kind, and it was indissolubly connected with witchcraft from the fourteenth century onwards.

[2] Written about thirty years before the Reformation.

with a naked sword. A head was then produced with three faces, representing the Triple Monad.

The magician opened his book, adored the triad and then prayed to the Devil till Satan appeared in person, gave him some money and promised more. The magician said it was not enough for his long service. The Devil answered, they must then find the help of a scholar, and so went to the prior of a monastery who was a Bachelor of Divinity and preacher of note. Why the Devil chose such a man is hard to say, unless he thought the mendicants were all rascals. However, the magician told the prior he had some wonderful manuscripts which he could not read and so desired his assistance.

He produced them : one an Old Testament, and the other a book on necromancy, which the scholar glanced at and said was a work of evil. The magician swore the prior to secrecy and then said he had more books, which, if interpreted, would make them both rich. The prior pretended to be caught and then wormed out of the magician the whole secret, even that concerning his possession of the Holy Thing which he kept under the bed.

The prior informed the authorities, the

magician, his wife, and daughter were arrested, the house was searched, the body of Christ was found and reverently carried away.

All that day and the next night the monks and priests prayed and chanted, and the next morning a special service was held in the cathedral. The streets were carpeted, the bells rang in all the steeples, the clergy walked in solemn procession—carrying their relics which they had rediscovered. The prior told the story from the pulpit to a great crowd, and in such detail that the vicar had to rebuke him. Two divines and two lawyers were brought from Paris to examine the prisoners. The magician was then put on the rack and confessed to horrors inconceivable, which included the confession that he was in league with the Devil, who was a constant visitor to his house at nights, which evidence was corroborated, in more detail than can be printed here, by both his wife and daughter.

Research into the psychology and folklore of witchcraft reveals some strange facts, and none more so than that the evidence concerning hallucination, superstition, and belief connected therewith was confined almost entirely to women. If, as might be assumed, these were but symptoms of hysteria common to the sex, our feelings may in charity turn from scorn or amusement to those of pity.

Illustrative of this, there is a remarkable record in M. Guizot's *Collection des Mémoires*. He relates how, at Nantes, a woman confessed to having been tormented by a demon who presented himself to her in a most attractive form. He addressed her in endearing language, but concealed his wicked intentions, and then gained her affections. When he had thus gotten control over her he performed the usual demoniac (Incubi) ceremony of initiation and recognition. . . . She had for her husband a brave soldier who for six years was kept in ignorance of the abominable alliance. During all this time the demon was her frequent companion.

In the seventh year, tortured by the reproaches of her conscience, she felt terrified, as much by the long course of infamy as by the fear of her Saviour, at the thought of Whom she trembled, lest His judgment should come suddenly upon her and she should be damned.

She therefore determined to confess her sins to the priest and change her conduct.

She visited the sacred shrines and implored the assistance of the saints, but no confession, no prayer, no almsgiving, could procure her consolation. Every day the demon subjected her to his attention, even more ardently than before. At length her disgrace became public, and her husband, hearing of it, looked upon her with horror.

Just at this time St. Bernard came into the district, and when the unhappy woman had knowledge of it she hastened to throw herself at his feet. Trembling, and in tears, she told him of her awful sufferings, which were very real to her, of the power of the demon to whom she was a prey, and how useless all her own efforts and those of the priests had been to overcome him. She added that her tormentor had informed her of his (St. Bernard's) arrival and had forbidden her with dreadful threats to visit him, saying that such proceedings would not avail her, for, as soon as the saint was gone, he, who had hitherto been her demon-lover, would become her most cruel persecutor.

The man of God, hearing these things, comforted the woman with words of mercy, and promised her the assistance of Heaven. As night was approaching, he directed her to trust in her Saviour and come to him on the morrow.

Accordingly, she visited him in the morning, but she was sad and downcast ; for the blasphemies and threats of the incubus who had been with her all the night had been worse than ever before.

" Have no fear for his threats," said St. Bernard, " but take my staff and place it handy in case he should again try to annoy you." The woman did as she was ordered, and when she went to rest that night she protected her couch with the sign of the cross and placed the staff beside her.

The incubus soon came, but daring not to approach or to molest her, contented himself by furious threatenings from a distance.

For the next Sunday the Holy Abbot had ordered that the people of the district be summoned to church by proclamation of the Bishop, and when the day came there was a large gathering at which St. Bernard, followed by two Bishops—Geoffrey of Chartres and Brieton of Nantes—entered the rood-loft, and having directed that all the attendants should hold lighted tapers in their hands, he then, along with the Bishops and the clergy, publicly exposed the wicked persecution of the demon ; afterwards, assisted by the priests and all the faithful present, he anathematised the evil spirit and forbade him in the name of Christ to approach any woman again.

When the sacred tapers were burnt out, the power of the demon became extinguished also. The woman then took the Sacrament ; and from that time onwards lived without either the demon or the hallucination. Hetero-suggestion, or, if you like, psycho-analysis, had killed both.

Whatever else the popular conception of witchcraft may have been, or still is, the fact remains that the witch enthusiasts were, above everything else, fanatics with a creed, and, albeit—as we have already endeavoured to show, for it is important—ardent disciples whose strength of faith was not unlike many religionists of a different order. And so confirmed were the witches in their own strange beliefs, and so strongly did they adhere to them that they were willing to endure most horrible tortures and to suffer death in defence of their actions and their faith.

Some explanatory distinction perhaps should be made here with regard to " witchcraft," so called, and " demoniacal possession," also so called. The two were invariably linked together when convictions were being pressed.

Witchcraft was considered a *voluntary* personal surrender to the Devil and an acquiescence in his will; being endowed with the power of divination, fortune-telling, horoscopy, the casting of spells, and other mysterious achievements; whereas, demonism or demoniacal possession was the *in*voluntary asylum given by anyone to demons or evil spirits. "Dæmon" was the name given by the ancients to any unseen, supernatural power, whether good or bad; but on the coming of Christianity the term was reserved for evil spirits, while the good spirits were termed "angels." Hence the terms "demonology" and "angelology."

In less enlightening times it was a characteristic to see in every event, even the most trivial, a direct supernatural interference wrought by the innumerable unseen messengers belonging to either one order or the other.

With the behaviour of demon-possessed humanity, the reader is probably familiar. The clearest instances are portrayed in the New Testament, and as every reader is acquainted more or less with the narratives there given, they have no need to be mentioned here. To-day the definition of " possession " is somewhat conjectural, but in nearly all the famous witch-trials, and especially in those that took place in America, the charges against those accused of witchcraft were made weighty and terrible by the inclusion of much fantastic but condemnatory evidence given as "*proof*" of demoniacal possession.

The belief in the possibility of being devil-possessed was an unarguable belief in the existence of a devil personified ; a devil with hairy body, cloven foot, horns, toasting-fork, and all the rest of the devilish paraphernalian make-up ; a devil with whom the witches could hold diabolical and incestuous communion ; a devil in whose possession there was a much-talked-about mystical black book with the names inscribed therein—in blood—of all those who had sworn allegiance to him !— and a lot more besides.

Suggestive of the popular imagination, even of the nineteenth century, there are the following lines. They appeared frequently, with little modification, and have been accredited to Richard Porson, Southey, and Coleridge,

" From his brimstone bed at the break of day
A-walking the Devil is gone,
To visit his little snug farm of the earth
And see how his stock goes on.
Over the hill and over the dale,
He walked, and over the plain ;
And backward and forward he swished his long tail
As a gentleman swishes his cane."

If the reader will take up any old book that
was published in the sixteenth or seventeenth
centuries, or even later, and glance at the
illustrations, he will understand why it was
that the idea of a devil-possessed world came
to be so impressed on the minds of the people.
Almost every pictorial page in any book,
sacred or otherwise, portrayed devils of every
conceivable description, until poor humanity
could not only see them, but could hear them
buzzing around, could see them in the dark,
could feel them, aye, and if reports are true,
could smell them.

Luther, if we are to believe the recorded
incident, saw the Devil in person and tried to
brain him with an inkpot. St. Dunstan on one
occasion got to such close quarters with him—
over a bit of love-making—that he was able to
get him by the nose with a pair of tongs and
hold him thus until he squealed for mercy ;
and others—saints, reformers, poets, drama-

tists, and authors, right up to the present
time—have taken a strange delight in present-
ing to us, with more or less success, the
imaginings of their own mind concerning " the
old 'un " and his make-up.   To-day, the ten-
dency is to connect him and his workings
—demoniacal possession—with spiritualistic
séances and such-like pastimes.

The old world had to acknowledge, as we
do to-day, that there was and is a very real
Power of Evil that had to be combated with,
and they naturally symbolised it in a personal
devil.   To show how these diabolistic ideas
cling to the fabric of memory and become
heirlooms of belief, it might be worth while
mentioning here how seventy or so years
ago the well-known Surrey Chapel at Blackfriars, London, was built octagonal shape so
that there would be no deep dark corners for
the Devil to hide in.—And now for the irony
of it.   A few years ago this chapel ceased
being used as a place of worship (in the orthodox sense).   It was sold by auction and
passed into the possession of pugilists and
prizefighters.   It is now known as " The
Ring."   Some worthy worldly folk believe
that the reason of its change from chapel to
boxing-ring is that the Devil, unable to find a

corner to hide in, scored over those who would confound him, by biding his time and then, as opportunity came, taking over the whole building, lock, stock, and barrel, so to speak.

This reminds one of the mediæval story of the monk who, fearing the Devil would carry him off, notwithstanding his efforts to combine goodness with merriment, entered into an agreement with him that he (the monk) could only be carried off if he was discovered asleep *between sheets*. The monk for a long while was able to dodge the evil day by an astute refusal to sleep in a bed at all, but one day when the Evil One made a call, he found the monk sitting in a chair—sound asleep—with an open manuscript book of theology on his lap. Here the Devil saw his opportunity. Quickly approaching the monk, he took hold of the open book, and then, raising it slowly until it was just under the sleeping monk's face, closed it with a BANG—with the monk's self-same head between its sheets. He had got him at last !

Around those old centuries what an exciting time the people must have experienced. At almost every turn, confronted as they were by all the infernal powers imaginable, it was no wonder that in their despair they could think of nothing better whereby to counteract the evil than to go through ceremonies of a simple innocuous character, believing, nevertheless, that in the doing of them they would frustrate the powers of darkness. The belief in the neutralising efficacy of ceremonial, the wearing of charms, amulets, necklaces, and so on, turns the key in a veritable Pandora-box of fantasy, which to this day, like our lucky black cats, lucky pigs, golliwogs, and billikins, is in our keeping, and will be handed down possibly to distant posterity.

That much of this ritual should, through its general adoption, have become merged into our daily thought and action as to pass notice —except to those of an inquisitive turn of mind, like folklorists, who reflect on this, that, and the other, and wonder *why* people do things—is not altogether surprising ; but the ritual is existent all the same.

Probably few people using the word " Abracadabra " as a verbal expression of surprise —instead of another useful though much maligned word of four letters—would recognise in it a connection with the bad old days of witchcraft ; yet in those times it played a truly significant part.

```
A B R A C A D A B R A
  B R A C A D A B R
    R A C A D A B
      A C A D A
        C A D
          A
```

Written triangularly on parchment and worn *next to the heart* it was considered a sure protection against spells, enchantments, etc.

```
A B R A C A D A B R A
A B R A C A D A B R
A B R A C A D A B
A B R A C A D A
A B R A C A D
A B R A C A
A B R A C
A B R A
A B R
A B
A
```

Another way of placing the letters was also given, and it will be observed that whereas in the previous collocation the word could be read across the top and downwards on the left-hand side of the triangle, in this it can be read across the top, up the right-hand side or along any line—if you continue upwards when arriving at the end of the line.

The charm is of Syrian origin, but has become world-wide in adoption. In literature the story is perpetuated how in 1588 a physician used the charm upon a patient suffering from fever, charged him £15 for it, and then made him eat it (the charm)—presumably to complete the cure.

Also for " raising the spell " much other queer ritual was indulged in. Some of it was as follows :

i. Following the witch home, plucking a handful of thatch from the roof of her dwelling, and burning it after it had been purified by a sprinkling of salt and water. The ashes would be buried at the change of the moon.

ii. Procuring a horseshoe that had been cast, dropping it in brine, and then nailing it, red-hot and with the horns uppermost, over the doorway.

iii. Putting salt, needles, pins, and three rusty nails in a bottle of salted water and preserving the same. This was also supposed *to make the witch suffer*. (The significance of the three nails was probably in regard to the connection they had with the crucifying of Christ.)

iv. To scratch the witch's arm with a pin, or to encourage a black cat to draw blood by scratching the arm of the bewitched. This may even have been one reason why the

witches adopted black cats—to have a mono-
poly of them and to make them artful so that
they would not draw blood.

If there was little chance of actually bleeding the witch, then the next best thing, it was
thought, was to do it symbolically by tying
red ribbons or red cotton round the arm of
whatever it was that had been "overlooked"
or "put upon." The wearing of the red
ribbon or cotton was supposed to raise the
spell besides acting as a preventive. When
there is a scare of smallpox in our own time
people get vaccinated and wear a red ribbon
round the arm "for further protection."
They have been known to wear the ribbon
without being vaccinated, such is their belief
in mascots.

v. In the North of England, at one time,
the people pinned their faith to the mountain-
ash, witch-hazel, and honeysuckle as antidotes
for witchcraft, and branches of the former
with sprays of the latter would be fastened
over the door of the dwelling-house and the
cattle-shed.

vi. "To prevent the witch, or hag"—as
an old chronicler puts it—"from entering the
stable, riding the mares, and keeping them in
a sweat all night (nightmare), a flint with

a hole in it should be hung round the mare's neck, or a cast horseshoe should be nailed above the door." According to Tacitus, the old witches of an exceedingly early period used to foretell events by listening to the whinnying or neighing of horses ; the forecast being suggested by the kind of sound audible. As bewitching spirits were thought to cling to the flowing mane and tail of the horse, so there arose the custom of tying up the mane in thirteen plaits and of tying the tail up short with a wisp of straw. This prevented them from being ridden at night. To this day horses with their manes plaited and tails tied up may be seen at any country fair or sale of horses. The more recent cutting of the mane and docking of the tail are mere survivals of the old custom, though probably few of those that have to do with horses know anything about it.

In England, as early as the year 747 the Ecclesiastical Courts were requested by Pope Gregory II to consider means for abolishing the cruel custom of cutting off horses' tails. But apparently, as the custom continued to prevail, owners of horses could not be persuaded to disbelieve the idea of bewitchment *via* the tail.

The hanging up of the horseshoe prevented witch-riding, or, as it was called in olden time, " nightmare."

vii. As a witch-spell (possession) was supposed to be caused by an evil spirit taking apartments in the heart or cranium of the person, various means were adopted to let it out or to capture and confine it when it did come out. Among primitive people, as many an old skull testifies, the demon was let out by trepanning. Among a later and less heroic people it was confined in the following manner. Some " water " belonging to the bewitched person would be placed in a bottle with a quantity of pins, needles and nails ; corked tight, and placed before a fire. So long as the bottle did not explode, the spirit was confined all right ; but as an old chronicler says : " It would often force the cork out of the bottle with a loud noise like that of a pistol, and cast the contents of the bottle *along with the spirit* to a considerable distance " !

viii. A family custom adopted for the purpose of circumventing a spell, was to make a cake of ginger, honey, pepper, and flour, into which would be dropped a small silver token. When the cake was baked it was cut up into as many pieces as there were members of the household, and five besides—Christ, the Virgin, and the three wise men. The pieces were then distributed and whoever found the coin would be " chaired." The " chairing " consisted of being lifted high above the heads of the assembly until the occupant of the chair could chalk a " + " on the ceiling. The " + " prevented—or was supposed to—any evil influence working, and remained on the ceiling until blackened out by smoke.

The sign of the cross was used because the Christians of the third century adopted it as a symbol of their belief in heavenly protection against subtle influences of the Evil One, and the idea, more beautiful then than in many a succeeding age, has never been lost sight of. When or before they undertook a journey it was their custom to make the sign of the cross on their body—for protection— just as some good people do to this day upon entering a church ; and furthermore, when a document was drawn up for the affixing of signatures those who were to sign it would, on writing their names, place a + after it, to preserve its provisions from going awry through the machinations of evil spirits. If for want of education a witness was unable

to write his name he would merely place a +
upon the document, which after all, was
thought to be of greater importance than the
signature itself. How many to-day, one
wonders, remember or know that when they
are placing a + to a document, or even a
ballot-paper, they are playing the part of
the legatee from a superstitious past.

So far have we travelled along the matter-
of-fact road of time that we have lost sight of
the real idea behind this and many another
universal custom.

This " cross " business might be further
pursued had we both the inclination and the
time, for in its simple mark could be found
the origin of other unlikely things of interest
besides such common symbols as crosses for
kisses and so on.

Possibly " shaking hands " with departing
friends is nothing more than the symbolic expression of the same old idea :—The hands
crossed : the sign of the cross to keep away
evil influences: Mizpah ! Good luck ! Swas-
tika !

The old superstition still remains, distorted
though it may be. The idea which gave it
birth has been forgotten in the events of a
more enlightened age, but much of the obser-

vance has been perpetuated until to-day by
the wearing of lucky charms and brooches in
the shape of " black cats " and " lucky pigs "
by quite intelligent people who know little
or nothing of the horrible significance these
things had in a more rugged and simple past.

Apparently the only time in all the year
when folk could walk about without fear of
witches' spells was at Christmas. An account
of the notion is given by Shakespeare when
he says :

> The cock that is the trumpet of the day
> Doth with his lofty and shrill sounding throat
> Awake the god of day ; and at his warning
> Whether in sea, or fire, in earth or air,
> The extravagant and erring spirit hyes
> To its confines, and of the truth therein,
> This present object made probation.
>   It faded at the crowing of the cock.
> Some say that ere against the season comes,
> Wherein our Saviour's birth is celebrated,
> The bird of dawning singeth all night long,
> And then, they say, *no spirit doth walk abroad.*
> The nights are wholesome, there no planet strikes,
> No fairy takes, *no witch hath power to harm,*
> So gracious and so hallowed is the time.

CHAPTER IX

WITCH-HUNTING CAMEOS

IN connection with witchcraft there are many surprising revelations; but none more so than that of witch-hunting—a sport followed with less compunction with regard to consideration for humane behaviour than rat-catching.

The partly-religious-partly-politic enthusiasts of the period of intensified witch-huntings —the seventeenth century—had read, or if they had not read, they had been told, how the Bible contained certain injunctions against witches: as for instance, in the Book of Exodus, where it is written: " Thou shalt not suffer a witch to live," or in Galatians, where witchcraft is mentioned along with heresies and seditions as works of the flesh and the Devil; or in the Chronicles, where it is recorded of Manasseh that " he did that which was evil. . . . He observed the times and used enchantments and witchcraft, and dealt with familiar spirits."

Then, coming to the injunction in Deuteronomy they read : " There shall not be found among you any one that useth divination, or an observer of the times, or an enchanter, or a witch, or a charmer, or a consulter with familiar spirits, or a wizard, or a necromancer." [1] This they took to heart as being meant especially for their guidance in dealing with those whom they judged as wizards.

It is also quite likely that the enthusiasts were imbued with the doings of that mighty witch-hunter, Jehu, who, as recorded in the Second Book of Kings, boasted of his " zeal for the Lord," and then, accusing Queen Jezebel of witchcraft, commanded that she

[1] In the Bible the terms witchcraft and sorcery are usually used in combination to designate the practice of the art of divination. One of the oldest of these practices was that of consulting with the dead. The spirit of the dead was known as " *ob*," and the consultation with such a spirit was accomplished by a woman who was called " the mistress of an *ob*." The earliest and indeed the most famous instance on record is that connected with King Saul, when on the night preceding the battle of Gilboa, in which he lost his life, he consulted the mistress of the *ob* at Endor, and Samuel's spirit was called up from the depths. It is thought that these mistresses or witches were proficient in the art of ventriloquism and that they simply impersonated the voice of the dead. Isaiah described them as those that " chirp and mutter."

should be thrown through a window to the
dogs howling in the street below. And of
how the self-same Jehu, suspecting seventy of
the king's sons of witchcraft, decapitated
them and stacked their heads on each side of
Jezreel's gates like so many bricks. And of
how he " slew all that remained of the house
of Ahab in Jezreel, and all his great men, and
his acquaintances, and his priests, until he
left none remaining."

These narratives concerning witchcraft, im-
perfectly understood, had no doubt a dire
effect upon the minds and the subsequent
action of seventeenth-century witch hunters
swayed more or less by emotion and religious fervour. They gradually changed from
being passive believers into ardent proselytes
and missionaries with a determination to overcome every obstacle imaginable ; stopping at
nothing, however horrible, in exterminating
" witches."

And there were others, who, seeing an
opportunity for battening on other peoples'
phantasms, did not let such an opportunity
slip by.

Chief of these was a lawyer named Matthew
Hopkins, who under the self-conferred title of
" Witch-finder General " travelled through

the counties of Essex, Norfolk, Huntingdon, and Suffolk "discovering witches," Bury St. Edmunds, Ely, and Chelmsford receiving special attention.

Procuring a kind of licence he was empowered to examine all those suspected of witchcraft by means of tortures which compelled them often to confess a guiltiness for most improbable and ofttimes impossible things ; which confessions invariably were as passports to the gallows.

So subtle was this Witch-finder General that he caused it to be put about that he had in his possession a certain pocket-book which he had cheated the Devil out of, and in it were the names of all the witches, as well as those of all the consulters of witches in England, whereby he was able to avail himself of exclusive information, necessary for carrying to a successful conclusion his super-witch-detective work. Really, it was not so very much unlike "The Black-book" of the political stunts of 1919 in which there was declared to be inscribed practically everybody that was anybody of importance in what was then "The Liberal Party." But that is another story!

In truth, this Hopkins was not only an impostor but a veritable inhuman monster of cruelty, and the wonder is that the inhabitants of Essex and the other counties to whom he was so attentive did not recognise in him the horrid symbol of the diabolical master whom he served and whose pocket-book he was supposed to have been in possession of.

He was the son of James Hopkins, Minister of Wenham, in Suffolk; by profession a lawyer practising in Ipswich. In 1644 he resided at Manningtree, a small place in the county of Essex. There with two assistants, one male, the other female, he busied himself with his persecutions. His mode of business was to travel with his assistants from one place to another—usually a town in which his spies had told him there were eccentric persons that had come under suspicion of either practising witchcraft or consulting with witches. To reimburse him for the expenses of the visit he would make a charge against the town's exchequer, and invariably he would get what he asked for. Aldeburgh in Suffolk paid him £6, and Stowmarket £23, and there is another record of Aldeburgh having paid his hangman eleven shillings for eleven hangings.

For downright heartless cruelty it would be difficult to equal Hopkins's method of working upon poor humanity when searching for

the proof of guilt—" the witches' mark."
" Trial by ordeal " in an earlier age, called
so because of the difficulty experienced in
trying to walk blindfolded between red-hot
ploughshares, was mild in comparison.

The Hopkins test was as follows : The
person accused of witchcraft, whether young
or old, good-looking or ugly, was stripped of
all clothing and made to sit cross-legged, much
like a working tailor, on a stool or table
placed in the centre of some old barn. If
there was any unwillingness shown by the
person on trial, binding with cords would be
resorted to. Then, long pins specially made
for the purpose would be pushed into the flesh
" to find the mark." This mark, which was
supposed to prove the bewitchment, was
believed to have been discovered if at the
moment the pin was stuck into any spot or
mole on the body the victim did *not* cry out
with pain. When one considers that the torture was carried on until there was most
probably an insensibility to *all* feeling, it is
easy to imagine that the witch-finder always
scored. And again, so wily was he, that to
make even more certain of discovering the
mark, a pricking instrument cleverly made on
the telescopic principle would be used, so

that when pressed against the flesh the point of it would disappear as though it had entered. This, of course, saved the victim a deal of physical pain ; but it gave a crooked verdict.

The mark having been found, it was vulgarly supposed that an imp would come to suck at it, so watch was kept through a hole in the door, and it never occurred but that the watcher confessed to having seen the imp at its work.

The truth is that more often than not " the mark " was just an ordinary mole, or in rare cases a small supernumerary *mamma*. The evidence of the watcher having seen the imp sucking at it was, of course, fiction.

In an old book, *The Lawes against Witches*, published in 1645, it is stated that the " witch hath some big or little teat upon her body where the Devil sucketh ; and besides sucking, the Devil leaveth upon their bodies other marks, sometimes like a blew spot. And on the meaner proselytes the Devil fixes in some secret part of their body a mark as his seal to know his own by. The part so stamped doth for ever after remain insensible, and doth not bleed, though ever so much pricked or nipped by thrusting into it a pin, awl, or bodkin." Readers of the author's book, *The Ghost-World*, will remember how in the ghost-story concerning the Duke of Buckingham mention is made of his having upon his body what was known as a " mark " or " witch's pap," etc.

However absurd such fancies may seem when reviewed in the light of present-day knowledge, and however captious we may be regarding the people of the bad old days who revelled in such fantasms, we must not lose sight of the fact that Alchemy, Horoscopy, Wizardry, and a kind of witchcraft not so bad as *the real thing* were then interwoven in the everyday lives of the great majority of people, and that they were spoken of—with and without their hideous appendages—in society in quite a free and easy manner even so late as the end of the eighteenth century.   For instance, in Congreve's celebrated play, *Love for Love*, which appeared at the Covent Garden Theatre in 1776, there is the following dialogue between an uncle, a nurse, and his niece :—

UNCLE (*to* NIECE).   Well, jill-flirt, you are very pert, and still ridiculing my celestial science.

NIECE.   Nay, Uncle, don't be angry ; for if you are I'll reap up all your false prophecies, ridiculous dreams, and idle divinations.   I'll swear you are a nuisance to the neighbourhood.   What a bustle did you make against the last invisible eclipse, laying in provision as 'twere for a siege !   What a world of fire and candle, matches and tinder-boxes did you purchase! One would have thought you were ever after to live underground.

UNCLE. Why, you malapert flirt——

NIECE. I'll declare how you prophesied popery was coming, only because the butler had mislaid some of the Apostle spoons. Indeed, Uncle, I'll indite you for a wizard.

UNCLE. Was there ever such a provoking minx?

NURSE (*entering*). Oh merciful father, how she talks!

NIECE. Hold! I can make oath on *your* unlawful midnight practices—you and the old Uncle.

NURSE. Heaven defend! I at midnight practices! Oh, Lord! What's here to do? I at unlawful doings with my master? Why, did you ever hear the like now?—Sir, did I ever do anything but warm your bed, and tuck you up, and set the candle and your snuffbox, and now and then rub the soles of your feet? Oh, Lord, I——

NIECE (*breaking in*). Yes, I saw you together, one night, through the keyhole, like Saul and the Witch of Endor, turning the sieve and the shears, and pricking your thumb to write poor innocent souls' names in blood. Nay, I know something worse, if I would only speak of it.

UNCLE. I defy you, hussy. But remember, I'll be revenged on you, cockatrice.

NIECE. Will you? I care not; but all be out then. . . . Look to it, Nurse; I can bring witness that you have a great unnatural teat under your left arm, and *he* another, and that you by turns suckle a devil, in the shape of a tabby-cat; so I can.

NURSE (*in horror*). A teat, a teat! I, an unnatural teat! Oh, the false, slanderous thing, feel here if I have anything but like another Christian.

Uncle. I will have patience, since it is the will of the stars I shall be thus tormented. . . .

(The dialogue ends with more of a similar character.)

To return to Hopkins. Another of his tests was that of "swimming the witch." It was an old, cruel custom, and the thought underlying it was probably that the pure element of water would not receive a person that had renounced baptism as the witches were said to have done, so that, if the person did not sink when dragged across the water, it proved her a witch.

The method of testing—"ordeal by water" —was to take the person to a pond and there tie the thumbs with string to the big toes. The person would then be placed in a sheet, the four corners of which would be loosely tied, and the whole placed on the edge of the water. The bundle would then be pulled across to the other side by a cord. If it floated—and it was more usual for the bundle, on account of its buoyancy, to float— the verdict was one of guilt, and the law was carried out accordingly.

If the "witch" *did* sink, and was dragged to the edge of the pond or river before life was extinct, and if, as was usually the case, the mob called for a further test, then other modes of torture were adopted, such as being kept without food for three or four days while sitting cross-legged, this being accompanied by a vexatious and continual watching, or else by an enforced wakefulness, either of which tortures in themselves, without counting certain indignities against the person, were enough to wring out a confession or in driving away the senses.

Another means of " proving " a witch was to get a big pair of scales and weigh her " against the Church Bible." If the suspected party weighed heavier than the Bible, well and good ; but if the Bible outweighed the witch, then the rectifying power of fire would be resorted to. Enforced confession was another means of arriving at a verdict. In many cases the expectation of torture so confused the mind that the person accused would confess almost anything—" to be done with it and get it over "—as one of them said. At a New England trial a number of women were *convicted upon confession*. Six of them, however, were liberated some time after and they then retracted their previous confessions in which they had admitted guiltiness, " for," said they, " what was the good of doing anything else when we were charged ? They told us we were witches, and they knew it, and we knew it, and they knew that we knew it, which made us think that it was so, and with our understanding, and our reason, and our faculties almost gone, we were not capable of judging our condition, and most of what we said was but a consenting to what they said."

" I went," says Sir George Mackenzie, in his work on *Criminal Law,* " when I was a Justice Depute, to examine some women who had confessed judicially. One of them told me that she had confessed, not because she was guilty, but that being a poor woman who wrought for her living, and, being defamed for a witch, she knew she would starve, for no person hereafter would give her food or lodging, and that all men would beat her and hound dogs at her, and that therefore she desired to be out of the world. Whereupon she wept most bitterly, and upon her knees called God to witness what she had said."

The extraordinary thing about these confessions was, that they were not confined to the simple, but that they were made by people of intelligence and even learning.

Richard Baxter, an eminent Nonconformist divine at the time of which we are thinking, was visiting some of the country jails, and he says he " spoke to pious, learned and credible persons " awaiting their end, and among them was an old Scripture reader named John Lowes, who for fifty years had been connected with the Church of Brandiston, near Framlingham in Suffolk. He was accused of being bewitched and of being possessed by two imps, one of which had sunk a ship just off the coast. This harmless old gentleman—eighty years of age—had come under the ban of Hopkins. The sentence seems to have turned upon his own confession of guilt, although it is quite likely he was a victim of political spite, so prevalent at that period of civil and religious unrest. He was a wonderful old fellow. At first, at the trial, he defended himself courageously, and was put back. Then he was put under watch and worried and tortured by being made to rush quickly across a room many times during the day and night with little respite until weary of life, and " scarce sensible of what he said or did," he confessed to having " sunk a ship off Ipswich with all its crew." He was placed in the jail of Bury St. Edmunds where there were nearly two hundred men and women under accusation.[1] He was executed with fifty-nine others, and so game was he to the last that on reaching the gibbet at the crossroads upon which he was to be judicially murdered, he stopped to " play the man," by reading aloud his own funeral service

The diabolical manner in which Hopkins played his part is almost incredible. On one occasion when evidence was desired against a number of associates of a woman who was known to attend witch-meetings, the said evidence was procured by the witch-hunters' confederate going in unto her at night-time, disguised as her familiar, and then betraying her into a confession. If it was not for the indelicacy of the subject many instances might here be given showing not only how the fears and the ecstasies of these deluded women ruled their lives and negatived all sense of decorum, but that the same influence also allowed them to become the willing tools of cunning men, even more depraved than themselves, who subjected them to frauds of a character as bad, if not

[1] In the counties of Essex and Suffolk, Hopkins was responsible for about 260 indictments, the greater number of which terminated in executions.

worse, than those which are related by Boccaccio in one of his books concerning the Angel Gabriel.

At the end of three years (1644–7) of witch-huntings, this Suffolk lawyer began to be found out, and the people of East Anglia commenced asking one another whether any section of the community was safe from his accusations or extortions ; and whether the time had not arrived to curb his lunatic ambitions.

One man who had wisdom and courage enough to tackle him was an obscure clergyman named Gaule, residing in Huntingdonshire. He wrote against the cruelties of witch-hunting in general and of Hopkins in particular, and preached against him as well.

He was a brave fellow taking great risks, and he knew it ; and the knowledge of it made him bolder still. When Hopkins became aware that he was being criticised, and hearing where the criticism came from, he showed again his sinister nature by writing to the important functionaries of Stoughton where Mr. Gaule lived, informing them that he (Hopkins) had " received an invitation to visit their town and to search for evil disposed persons called witches." He also intimated that he had heard " the minister of the place through ignorance was against him " ; but that " God willing, he intended to hear that minister's singular judgment in and on the behalf of such parties," etc.

He also asked "whether the place of Stoughton afforded many sticklers for such cattell," and whether it would give him and his assistants " upon our arrival, good welcome and entertainment as other towns have done where I have been ? Or else I shall betake me to such places where I do and can punish without control but *with thanks and recompense.*"

So far as is known, the dignitaries of Stoughton, to their honour, diplomatically treated the General's request with stony silence. It would be interesting, to-day, to know how they discussed it at their municipal gathering.

By documentary evidence one gathers that soon after this there was further opposition, and that both Hopkins and his business were getting towards the rocks, for early in 1677 he resorted to advertising in the following manner (although at the same time it may have been intended as a counterblast against the opposition). However, he resorted to publishing pamphlets, the contents of which may be judged by the labels or title-pages. One of which was :—

The Discovery of Witches
In answer to Several Queries lately delivered
To the Judges of the Assizes
For the County of Norfolk

and now published
By
MATTHEW HOPKINS

The Witchfinder-General
For the Benefit of

THE WHOLE KINGDOM.

1677.

There is a saying, however, that " you can fool all the people some of the time, and some of the people all the time, but you can't fool all the people all the time," and this seems to have been proved with regard to Hopkins. Even the above pamphlet did not save him. A month or so afterwards he was seized by an indignant and long-suffering country-folk, who, believing that one bad turn deserved another, with rough justice put him to his own test of " swimming." Like many a witch in a similar predicament, instead of sinking, he happened to float. So he was adjudged by the same ruling as that by which he had sent so many others to the scaffold. He was hanged as a wizard.[1]

[1] Although the term witch applied to either women or men, the latter were generally referred to as wizards.

CHAPTER X

A TYPICAL ENGLISH WITCH-TRIAL

THE WITCHES OF BURY ST. EDMUNDS [1]

ON a spring morning in the year 1622 the old-world town of Bury St. Edmunds in the County of Essex, England, was all agog with excitement on account of a witch-trial that was about to take place in the old court-house adjoining the market-place.

The noise coming from the unlocking and the unbolting of the court-house door denoted to all and sundry that the performance was about to commence. The witnesses according-ly take their places in the mouldy room ; the jurymen have been called and—like

---

[1] An account of this particular trial has been given here because during the witch-mania in America it was frequently referred to for the information which it con-tained, and which was thought to be reliable enough to be taken as a guide for the framing of the witch-trials there. A brief account of witchcraft in America is given in Chapter XI.

sheep—ushered into their pen of a jury-bench. In tense excitement and with faces indicative of rustic wonder, they one and all await events.

Another door opens, and, simultaneously with many a buzfuz and bigwig, two women, one old, haggard and fearful, the other middle-aged, make their appearance.

Their names are called—Amy Duny and Rose Cullender, and they are severally indicted for bewitching Ann Durent, Elizabeth Durent, William Durent, Jane Bocking, Susan Chandler, Elizabeth and Deborah Pacy.

The evidence whereon they are to be tried stands upon divers particular circumstances and is as follows :

(1) That Ann Durent, Susan Chandler and Elizabeth Pacy, when on an occasion of their coming into court at a previous hearing were bewitched so that they fell into strange fits, and were unable to give their depositions.

(2) Evidence was given by Ann Durent to the effect that having to go away from home for a few hours she left to the care of Amy Duny her little child, and that when she did return home Amy Duny told her that the child had cried and so to quieten it she had given it suck ; whereat she expressed her

displeasure. After which Amy Duny went away and as she went she did cast a spell by her discontents and menaces.

(3) This was followed the night after by the child falling into strange fits, wherein it continued for divers weeks. A doctor, Jacob by name, advised the mother to hang up the child's bedclothes in the chimney corner and to let them remain there all day, and then at evening when she got them down for the putting of the child to bed, to look into them, with the further advice that if she found anything strange there to throw it without fear into the fire.

Accordingly when the clothes were taken down and looked into, "out there fell a great toad, which did *run* quickly up and down the hearth"—(fancy a toad *running*!). A boy catching it did hold it over the fire with a pair of tongs, where it made a horrible noise, and flashed like gunpowder, and exploded into a report like that of a pistol, whereupon it was to be seen no more.

(4) The next day a kinswoman of Amy Duny told the witness (Ann Durent) that she had an aunt all grievously scorched by the fire, and upon witness going to her house she found her in just such a condition.

The scorched old lady then told her that Amy Duny (one of the witches) had said it " served her right," or that she might " thank her for it," and that she would live to see some of her children dead, and herself upon crutches (another spell).

(5) This witness (Ann Durent) also testified that another child of hers, the aforesaid Elizabeth Durent of the age of eleven years, was also taken with fits as William was, and that when she was in these fits she did complain much of the manner in which Amy Duny did appear to her, and did afflict her.

(6) The witness also alleged to the finding of Amy Duny in her house one day when she had not been invited there. She had therefore pushed her out, and when she had done so the accused turned round upon her and did cast a spell, saying : " You need not be so angry, your child won't live long."— Within three days the child died.

(7) She also said, that she herself was not long afterwards taken with such lameness in both her legs, that she was forced to go upon crutches. Indeed, now that she was in court she was upon them.

This last witness coming to the end of her evidence, resumed her seat, and Elizabeth

Pacy, aged eleven, with her sister, aged nine, were called upon to tell what they knew against the accused. " All the truth, and nothing but the truth ! "

(8) The elder child was in court, but in consequence of Amy Duny's spell, had been— as it was declared—made utterly speechless, and at times utterly senseless. To test the truth of this statement, and the genuineness of the affliction, the judge directed that the accused be brought to Elizabeth in a manner not noticeable by the child, and made to touch her from behind. The idea being that if the woman accused was not " possessed " of evil influence, the child would not be aware as to who it was that had touched her. Upon feeling the touch, however, the child immediately turned round and leaped upon the prisoner in a frenzy, thus indicating " possession."

(9) The younger sister, Deborah, was represented by her father, who testified to her being too unwell to come to the court on account of Amy Duny " grumbling at her." The grumbling had been of such a character that shortly afterwards the child had been taken with extreme pain in her stomach, like the pricking of pins, and with shrieking

in a dreadful manner, like a whelp, rather than a rational creature.

(10) The physicians were unable to conjecture any cause for the fits other than that Amy Duny was a woman of ill-fame and had affrighted the child with the apparition of her person.

(11) Upon one occasion when Amy Duny had been punished by being placed in the stocks, she was heard to say : " Mr. Pacy keeps a great stir about his child ; but let him have to do as much by his children as I have done by mine." On being asked what she had done to her children, she replied : " I have had to open my child's mouth with a wooden tap to give it victuals." The witness added that within two days of this the fits of his daughter were so bad that they could not preserve either breath or life without the help of a tap. And that both his children cried out that they were being tormented and afflicted by the apparitions of Amy Duny and Rose Cullender.

(12) The fits of the children were various. " They would sometimes be lame on one side, then on the other. Sometimes they would be deaf, dumb, or blind for a long while together. Upon recovery of their speech they

would cough violently and vomit crooked pins.
At one time it was a tuppeny nail with a
very broad head ! " *Commonly at the end of
every fit they would* cough up pins.—It was
considered a sure sign of bewitchment or
possession.

(13) When the children read they could
not pronounce the name of " Lord " or
" Jesus " or " Christ " (this was also considered a sign of bewitchment—it denoted
a belief in the power of Satan as being con-
trariwise or stronger than the power of
Christ) ; but at the attempt they would fall
into fits, and say : " Amy Duny says I must
not use that name." When they came to
the name of " Satan " or " Devil " or " Beelzebub," they would clap their fingers on the
book and cry out : " This bites, but it makes
us speak right well ! " The children in their
fits would often cry out : " There stands Amy
Duny or Rose Cullender " ; and they would
afterwards relate " that those witches appearing before them did threaten them. That if
they told what they saw or heard, they would
torment them ten times more than ever they
did before."

This last witness (the father of the afflicted
children) having concluded his evidence, his

place was taken by Margaret Arnold, his sister.

(14) Margaret Arnold testified unto the like sufferings of the children at her house, whither her brother had brought them. And that "sometimes they would see things like mice, but which were not mice, running about the house. One day one of them suddenly snapped one up with the tongs, and upon throwing it into the fire, it screeched out like a rat. At another time, a thing like a bee— but it wasn't a bee—flew into the face of the younger child : whereupon the child fell into a fit and at last vomited up a tuppeny nail with a big broad head to it."

She further corroborated her brother's evidence by affirming that " the thing like a bee which came from the witches and flew in the child's face, did bring the nail and did force it into the child's mouth."

The child would in like manner be "assaulted with flies, which would bring crooked pins unto her, making her first swallow them and then vomit them up."

She one day, herself, " caught an *invisible* mouse, and throwing it into the fire it exploded like gunpowder. None *besides the child saw the mouse, but everybody saw the flash* " !

Margaret Arnold having finished her evidence, " the truth and nothing but the truth," stood down, and the father of Ann Durent (grandfather to the children) stood up to continue the tale.

(15) He said that upon a discontent of Rose Cullender, his daughter was taken with much illness in the stomach, and great sore pains, like the pricking of pins, and then with swooning fits, from which recovering, she declared she had seen the apparition of Rose Cullender, the witch, threatening to torment her. She likewise vomited up diverse pins. The girl was present in court when the trial opened, but upon Cullender looking upon her with her evil eye, she fell into fits, as made her utterly unable to declare anything.

(16) Another witness, Ann Baldwin, testified to the truthfulness of the last witness's statements.

(17) Evidence was now called in support of the charge of bewitching Jane Bocking ; as the said Jane was said to be too weak to appear at the Assizes, her place was taken by her mother. She declared that her daughter having formerly been afflicted with swooning fits, and recovered from them, was now taken with great pains in her inside and

new swooning fits. That she took very little food, but every day vomited crooked pins. In her first fits she would extend her arms and strike postures as if she were catching at something that was not there, and when her clutched hands were forced open, they would find several pins, diversely crooked, unaccountably lodged there. She would also maintain a discourse with someone who was *invisibly* present. When casting about her arms she would say: " I will not have it!" but after a time she would say: " Then I will have it!" and would close her hand very tightly. When opened later, a large lath-nail was found therein. Her great complaint, however, was that she was visited by the shapes of Amy Duny and Rose Cullender.

(18) Another " bewitched," Susan Chandler, not being in court, her mother gave evidence on her behalf.

She said that her daughter was one day concerned because Rose Cullender had touched her upon the head, after which she fell very sick, and in the night she did cry out that the witch had come to her bed; and as the fits grew upon her she got violent and said that Rose Cullender had not come by herself but that she had brought a great dog with her. She had also vomited up crooked pins, and when she had come to the court she had fallen into fits, so had to be taken home. She also stated that she herself was present when the witch, Rose Cullender, was searched, and that on a certain part of her body the searchers found a thing like a teat, of an inch long ; a little lower down they found three smaller ones. At the end of the long teat there was a little hole, and it appeared as if it had been newly sucked [1] ; upon straining it a little milky fluid issued out.

The daughter, Susan Chandler, was here seen to be in court, so she was asked if she had recovered and whether she was in a condition to take oath and give evidence. She said " Yes," and was duly sworn. She, however, fell into a most violent fit, crying out " Burn her ! Burn her ! " so that she had to be taken away.

The father, who was in court, testified to all the mother had said, with the exception of the search and the discovery of the witches' mark.

The evidence here, seemingly, having come

[1] This is in accordance with the old belief that witches gave suck to imps, etc.

to an end, Mr. Sargeant Keeling courageously remarked, notwithstanding the popular feeling towards the accused, that " *the evidence was not sufficient* to convict *the prisoners.*"

" For," he said, " admitting the children were bewitched, yet it can never be applied unto the prisoners upon the imagination only of the parties afflicted ; inasmuch as no person whatsoever could then be in safety."

Here the case would have closed and the verdict no doubt have gone in the prisoners' favour, had there not been in the court, watching the proceedings, a remarkable and learned doctor from Norwich—Sir Thomas Browne— who being called to give his opinion, said that " the fits were natural, but heightened by the Devil co-operating with the malice of the witches at whose instance he did the villainies. He therefore believed the persons were bewitched," and added that " in Denmark there had lately been a great discovery of witches who used the very same manner of afflicting people : by conveying pins and nails into them. The Devil in witchcraft did work upon the bodies of men and women, upon a natural foundation, and that he did extraordinarily afflict them with such distempers as their bodies were most subject to," etc.

Needless to say, the learned doctor's testimony helped to heap coals of fire on to the heads of the poor women being tried for their lives. The flagging evidence against them was now resuscitated, and further malicious charges were brought forward.

(19) It appears the two women on one occasion had gone to buy some fish, and as the fishmonger attempted to play the part of the profiteer they bluntly retaliated by that process commonly known as " ticking him off." In the rough language of their day they told him to go to a place where there is perpetual summer heat—or for that matter, anywhere else he pleased, and they also made him to understand that it was their wish for the Devil to take him and his money as well, and the whole of his fishy family and all his friends. The spell seems to have worked, for soon after this a carter delivering something in the neighbourhood drove his cart up to the door of the cottage where the women lived, and was bewitched so that " the cart remained unmovable between and without touching the gateposts, and the horse, try as much as it could, was able neither to go backward nor forward."

(20) A farmer, Robert Sherringham, now

came forward and testified that when passing Rose Cullender's house the axle-tree of the wagon in which he was riding broke, and that as the wagon knocked the corner of her house, she came out in anger and vehemently threatened him, saying his horses should suffer for it. Within a short time all his four horses died; after which he sustained many other losses in the sudden dying of his cattle. He himself was taken with a lameness in his limbs, and so vexed with insects of an extraordinary number and bigness on his clothing that no art could hinder the swarming of them till he burnt up two suits of apparel.

(21) Then another witness came, swearing that he had heard Amy Duny say "the Devil would not let her rest until she were revenged on the wife of a Cornelius Sandswel."

(22) Cornelius Sandswel testified that his wife's poultry died suddenly after Amy Duny had cast her spell over them, and also the chimney of their cottage had fallen down after the same Amy Duny had said it was to do so.

The evidence against the accused having now come to an end, the judge (Mr. Justice

Hale, afterwards Sir Matthew Hale) sums up.

Turning to the twelve good men and true, he tells them they are to decide from the evidence they have heard, first, whether the children were bewitched, and secondly, whether the prisoners at the bar were guilty of it. To help them in their decision, he said that he made no doubt himself but that there were such creatures as witches; for the Scriptures affirmed it, and the wisdom of all the nations had provided laws against such; but he prayed the God of Heaven to direct their hearts in the weighty thing they had in hand; for " to condemn the innocent, and let the guilty go free, were both an abomination of the Lord."

The jury gave it their consideration. In half an hour they let the judge know that their verdict was " Guilty upon all the several indictments " !

The two women were then condemned, and duly executed in the market-place of Bury St. Edmunds.

The morning after the women were condemned, the afflicted children, with their parents, called upon the judge at his lodgings to tell him they were now in as good health as ever before in their life : being restored within an hour of the time that the witches were sentenced.

CHAPTER XI

WITCHCRAFT IN AMERICA

A S the practice of witchcraft in America and the methods adopted there for its suppression were so very similar to those in Britain, the following short account may not be without interest.

" Witchcraft, which is fellowship by covenant with a familiar spirit, to be punished with death. Consulters with witches not to be tolerated, but either to be cut off by death or banishment or other suitable punishment "—so ran the American law against witchcraft in the middle of the seventeenth century.

Yet, until 1692 or thereabouts it was only noticeable by spasmodic outbreaks of little or no importance. It became very prevalent during the next dozen years.

Carried over by emigrants from the Mother Country to the Puritanical colony of New England, it settled itself for an incubation period—strangely enough—in the village of

Salem, County *Essex*,[1] Massachusetts, and in this place, as events afterwards proved, there occurred some of the most remarkable trials in the whole story of witchcraft.

Two men whose names are linked up more than any other with the witch-trials of this period are those of Sir William Phipps and Cotton Mather.

Sir William Phipps was the Governor of the colony. He left London for Massachusetts in the early part of 1692, and took part in the trials which commenced in June of the same year. That he was sent over from England on purpose to superintend these trials is not known for certain ; but in all probability he was.

He left his native land at a time when there was a tremendous witch-hunt and a most complete system of persecution had been indulged in, so that his intimate knowledge of evidence for defending those accused should have stood him in good stead had he espoused the idea of counteracting with common sense and strong will the charges upon which so many harmless women and

[1] It was in the English county of Essex that Hopkins the Witchfinder-General commenced his persecution of witches.

old men, aye, and youngsters too, were to be sent to their death.

But however good his intentions may have been, the fates were against him. His best-laid plans—if he had any—to save the community, and himself, from an everlasting shame were dissipated by popular frenzy and mobocracy.

Of Phipps's companion, Cotton Mather, we will speak later.

Besides those unfortunate people who were accused extraordinarily by mobs and hanged on trees, it is to be feared that many who were even tried judicially, " proved," and condemned as witches, were no witches at all, but that they were mere victims of narrow-minded prejudice and bigoted judgment. As, for instance, the charge brought in Long Island, just prior to the general outbreak, against a woman named Mary Wright, who was arraigned on the capital charge of witch-craft and of " being suspected of dealings with the Evil One."

Long Island, feeling itself unable to adjudicate in a satisfactory manner, had the case transferred to the Court of Massachusetts, where it was declared that charges of this sort were more common and *the proofs neces-*

sary to support them—the charges—were better understood ! The result, however, contrary to expectations, was that on the charge of witchcraft she was acquitted ; but for happening to belong to that sect known as Quakers, she was convicted and banished from within the jurisdiction of the court.

Just as Egypt in days of old had its witch-hunter in the person of Jehu, the Continent in his Holiness Pope Pius, England in Hopkins the witchfinder-general, and Scotland in King James, so America had its witchfinder in the Reverend Cotton Mather.

Cotton Mather was born in Boston in 1662 of Nonconformist parents—both his father and grandfather being Congregational ministers. His mother was the daughter of a minister named Cotton. Thus it would seem that young Cotton Mather inherited a double share of piety which, as after-events proved, he was unable to counterbalance by the necessary amount of wisdom needed at all times for judging one's fellow-creatures aright.

Like other notorious personages mentioned in these pages, he chose as his forte in life that of hunting witches, and he seems to have applied the art with an assiduity and a perseverance worthy of a better cause.

Such an eye and such a mind had he at the age of thirty for spotting devils, that on one occasion when he was fasting and preaching on behalf of a damsel who was said to be " possessed," he " saw " the devil that was in the girl fly out at him, and then on to the page of the open Bible from which he was reading, tearing it right across the 33rd verse of the 8th chapter of St. Mark's Gospel, the rendering of which, if the reader does not remember it, is : " Get thee behind me, Satan : for thou savourest not the things that be of God."

Some years earlier he had been acquainted with a Boston family named Goodwin, in which there had been the usual performances of deceit and credulity suggestive either of cunning or imbecility, and which indeed should have been interpreted as such, and would have been by all except the zealous fanatics of the period who preferred to accept it as evidence of bewitchment needing the purifying powers of fire or the gallows for its correction.

The Goodwin family, it so happened, were, like Cotton Mather's family, very pious ; but their piety as judged by themselves was of a very different value. The Goodwins believed themselves to be so unworthy of heavenly grace as to be abandoned to the whims of all the devils imaginable, while Cotton Mather's estimation of himself was that he was Heaven's chosen messenger endowed with power from on high to hunt out and destroy all those upon whom, like the Goodwins, he imagined he saw the brand that marked them for the burning. So paradox meets paradox.

Thus it came about that when Bridget Bishop, an old charwoman, roundly abused the Goodwins because they had accused her of stealing some family linen, they needs must so take it to heart as to believe themselves to be good-for-nothing mortals, and then wilfully misbehave themselves in various ways, as though they were really and truly bewitched.

The Goodwin children, who must have been trained in the ways they were to go and had evidently been well schooled in the performances of the bewitched, were soon afterwards observed—so it was declared—to assume astounding physical contortions, which could only be attributed to Satan. Every joint from little finger to big toe became disjointed. They then went deaf and dumb, and blind by turns. Their tongue would be pulled out

by unseen spirits and then as quickly let go,
and it would rebound with a snap! They
would be burned by hot irons which could
only be felt and not seen. They would be
beaten and cut at unmercifully by spiritual
demons until they whined and writhed with
pain—and much more of a similar character.

The clergy of the district, becoming anxious,
met at the house of the Goodwins for prayer
and fasting. It was at this stage in the
proceedings that Cotton Mather came upon
the scene.

As the exhortations and fastings were unable to raise the spell, recourse was had to
the local stipendiary. The old charwoman,
being accused as the author of all the trouble,
was arrested. She was summarily charged,
but as she would neither deny nor confess
her guilt to her judges, she was ordered to be
examined " very strictly," so that it might be
known whether she was a witch or whether she
was in any way "crazed in her intellectuals."

One would have thought there was a loop-
hole here through which she might have
escaped; but no. So intelligently did she give
her replies to their questions that she was
deemed to be quite sane, and *therefore* guilty
of the charge of witchcraft. She was accord-

ingly sentenced to death, and duly hanged on Gallows Hill, outside Salem, Massachusetts.

Before the death sentence was carried out, she was frequently visited by Cotton Mather ; not with the idea of saving her poor life, it is to be feared, but with the object of adding to his knowledge—as in King James's case— so that he might be able the more exactly to pursue what he considered to be his righteous way. If curiosity was the object of his visits he must have been mightily satisfied with the result, for the condemned woman informed him most emphatically— with her tongue in her cheek, and with much detail—that she was all he supposed her to be, and that the Devil, whom she considered to be her master, had never relaxed his attentions to her, and also she believed he never would.

The records give it that Cotton Mather made no effort on the woman's behalf, but that he accompanied her to the scaffold as if to make sure of her getting her deserts.

Whether the people of New England con- sidered themselves fortunate or otherwise in their possession of such a zealous witch- eradicator will probably never be known for certainty ; but sure it is that to Cotton

Mather the dire work of extirpation was very necessary, and that he was not wanting in the assurance of his own ability to carry through the self-imposed task.

Like other notorious witch-hunters, he had his own ideas for stamping out the disorder. Assuming a kind of dictatorship over all and sundry, he broadcasted news concerning what he styled the afflicted state of his poor neighbours, suffering by molestations from the invisible world, at the same time apprehending it as deplorable, and calling for the utmost help of all persons in their several capacities to assist him.

These efforts stimulated amongst the ignorant people and those possessed of religious melancholia a belief in " devil possession " to a degree until then little dreamed of, with the result that a great impetus was given to the witch-huntings. People of respectable position all over the state who had hitherto lived irreproachable lives now became suspect. Charges were made, and condemnation followed so quickly that in less than a month six persons were executed.

In another month five more had shared the same fate, and among them was a devout minister of the Gospel : a Mr. George Burroughs, whose principal crime seems to have been, *not* that he believed in witchcraft, *but that he disbelieved in it*, and had even had the courage to say so.

His fate excited considerable interest and sympathy, which was checked at the place of execution by Cotton Mather, who happened to be present on horseback. Standing up in the stirrups he addressed the sympathising crowd, and assured them that the man on the gallows was an impostor.

With Burroughs there was executed a man named John Willard, who strangely enough had been employed previously to arrest some of those persons who had been charged with witchcraft. He in turn had been accused and arrested because from conscientious motives he had refused to arrest any more. He had attempted to save himself by flight ; but had been overtaken.

A few days after this, seven more unfortunate victims were hanged at the same place, and one, in accordance with the old criminal law, was *pressed* to death for refusing to plead.

About the same time, on a single day, on the same Gallows Hill, no fewer than five women were executed in a group, while at the same place and time there were six others awaiting their turn for similar treatment and many more in jail awaiting trial.

That the conviction pleased him there can be no doubt for he issued a leaflet in which he declared :

" We cannot but with thankfulness acknowledge the success which the Merciful God has given to the sedulous and assiduous to defeat the abominable witch-crafts which have been committed in this country ; humbly praying, that the discovery of those mysterious and mischievous wickednesses may be perfected. We have seen an horrible thing done in our Land ! O 'tis a most humbling thing, to think, that ever there should be such an abomination among us, as for a crue of humane race, to renounce their Maker, and to unite with the Devil, for the troubling of mankind, and for people to be (as it is by some confess'd), Baptized by a Fiend using this form upon them, ' Thou art mine, and I have a full power over thee ! ' afterwards communicating in an Hellish Bread and Wine, by that Fiend administred unto them. It was said in Deut. 18. There shall not be found among you an Inchanter, or a witch, or a Charmer, or a Consulter with Familiar Spirits, or a Wizzard, or a Necromancer ; For

all that do these things are an Abomination.
Alas, that New-England now should have
these Abominations in it. Alas, what Humili-
ations are we all hereby oblig'd unto ? O
'tis a Defiled Land, wherein we live.

" Satans prevalency of this Age, is most
clear in the marvellous Number of Witches,
abounding in all places. Now Hundreds are
discovered in one Shire ; and, if Fame
Deceives us not, in a Village of Fourteen
Houses in the North, are found so many of
this Damned Brood. Yea, and those of both
Sexes, who have Professed much Knowledge,
Holiness, and Devotion, are drawn into this
Damnable Practice.

" I pray, let not New-England become of an
Unsavoury and a Sulphurous Resentment in
the Opinion of the World abroad, for the
Doleful things which are now fallen out among
us "—together with much more similar clap-
trap.

A further increase in the hangings and the
crushings followed, but it caused the magistrates who had conducted previous proceedings to get alarmed, and to have some doubts
as to the wisdom of allowing such a state of
affairs to continue. The Governor of Massachusetts called upon Cotton Mather to give

justification for what had been done. In reply he gave an elaborate account of the trials at Salem, comparing them with those in other parts of the world, and especially with England.

Possibly the justices would have suppressed Cotton Mather, but they were fearful of opinion.

At this very time the wife of the minister of a place called Beverley was made to take her place among others accused of being passive against the witches. Her husband, Hales by name, had, during the previous months been, like Mather, an enthusiastic promoter of prosecutions, but as the injustice of the whole proceedings in which he was a willing accomplice had been brought home to him he began to waver in his zeal and belief. Now to his horror he found his own wife arrested and that other ministers present at the charge were not willing to believe in the possibility of error, and even raised a question of conscience ; *whether the Devil could not assume the shape of an innocent and pious person—such as the lady on trial—* for the purpose of afflicting his victims.

It may readily be perceived that under such argument as this no one's life was safe.

At the same time a justice of the peace, named Bradstreet, for refusing to issue further warrants against the people of a place known as Andover, because the jail there was already far too full, was himself suspected of witchcraft, cried out upon and accused of having killed nine people by means of spells. So alarmed was he that he fled from the place, thus saving his life.

The accusers, incensed at losing their prey, now began to aim at others of even higher position in society, until at last they loaded their stunt-camel with the proverbial last straw in the shape of an accusation against no less a personage than Lady Phipps—the Governor's wife ; this charge, however, did not materialise.

The deathblow to the disreputable business seems to have been given—according to Cotton Mather—by a Boston gentleman, who, when cried out upon, counter-attacked his accusers in double quick time by obtaining a writ of arrest against them for defamation of character ; laying the damage at a thousand pounds, which, in those " good old days," was a fairly respectable amount.

The accusers, strange as it may seem, took fright. Many who had made confessions retracted them; consequently all accusations fell into disrepute. The Governor Phipps and his wife returned to old England; the people generally returned to a state of sanity, and the witch-huntings shortly afterwards began to fizzle out.

The witch-hunting fever in America definitely subsided a short time afterwards when a judge, sitting at the court of Charlestown, was confronted by quite a respectable old lady of eighty, who was made to make her stand because she had admonished an evil-doer by saying: " God would not prosper him (the evil-doer) if he wronged the widow." The judge looked on this woman with a deal of pity, saying he did not know who it was that obstructed the execution of justice by such proceedings, but that he knew thereby the Kingdom of Satan was advanced, and so " would the Lord have mercy on this Country." He then cleared by proclamation all those others that were in prison of charges made against them, and declined any more to take his seat in court.

One does not know for certain, but it is more likely than not that many of those unfortunate people who were arraigned for witchcraft were completely innocent of the charges brought against them. They were there as " those practising witchcraft," to be humiliated and degraded more because they happened to be Quakers than for any other reason, possibly ; and the proceedings against them on counts of witchcraft were but a continuation of the persecution that they had long been subjected to in one form or another.

Orthodox " Histories " do not throw much illumination on this phase of the humanities, but some old documents or pamphlets written at that period do. Occasionally we come across one and it portrays in no unmistakable manner the agony of soul behind the printed word, but withal a wonderful determination to endure all things to the end, even imprisonment and death.

For fear one of these old human documents has never come the way of the reader, and perhaps never will, here is an announcement of the publication of one of them giving in cold print words that must have burned deep into the heart and mind of George Bishope, its author. They indicate better than any words of the writer to what degree of ferocity the persecution was pressed. The announcement is as follows :

"NEW ENGLAND JUDGED, Not by Man's but the Spirit of the Lord: and The Summe sealed up of the New-England's Persecutions, being A Brief Relation of the Sufferings of the People called Quakers in . . . America, from . . . the Fifth Moneth 1656 (the time of their first Arrival at Boston from England) to the . . . Tenth Moneth, 1660, wherein the Cruel Whippings and Scourgings, Bonds and Imprisonments, Beatings and Chainings, Starvings and Huntings, Fines and Confiscation of Estates, Burning in Hand and Cutting of Ears, Orders of Sale for Bond-men, and Bond-women, Banishment upon Pain of Death, and Putting to Death of those People, are Shortly touched ; with a Relation of the Manner, and some of the Other most Material Proceedings ; and a judgement thereupon, in Answer to a certain Printed Paper, intituled, A DECLARATION OF THE GENERAL COURT OF THE MASSACHUSETS holden at Boston the 18, October, 1658 ; also an Appendix ; being CERTAIN WRITINGS OF THOSE PERSONS WHICH WERE THERE EXECUTED, together with a short Relation of the Tryal, Sentence, and Execution of VViliam Leddra, Written by Them in the time of their Imprisonment, in the Bloody Town of Boston, 1661."

CHAPTER XII

WITCHCRAFT PHANTASMAGORIA

A STRANGE fact concerning the charges of witchcraft was that they became, by easy stages, according to the change of mental outlook, a kind of religious and political " test." An ardent enthusiast of one political party, or a bigot belonging to a particular religious sect, had only for the gratification of malignant spite to bring such a charge against another, and that individual was got rid of in the most effectual manner possible.

And, at the hands of the common people " the witch " did not fare much better. Such was the general condition of the time that any old man or woman, deformed by age and want—and especially if they happened to be a little eccentric or spiteful—was considered a fit and proper person upon whom the charge could be laid. The Elizabethan dramatist, William Rowley, reflects this tenor of mind in one of his plays, where he makes an old

woman exclaim, when she is called a witch for
picking up sticks :

> Why should the envious world
> Throw all their scandalous malice upon me ?
> 'Cause I am poor, deformed, and ignorant,
> And like a bow bent and buckled together
> By some more strong in mischief than myself ;
> Must I for that be made a common sink
> For all the filth and rubbish of men's tongues
> To fall and run into ? Some call me Witch,
> And being ignorant of myself, they go
> About to teach me how to be one : urging
> That my bad tongue—by their bad usage made so—
> Forespeaks their cattle, doth bewitch their corn,
> Themselves, their servants, and their babes at nurse :
> This they enforce upon me : and in part
>   Make me to credit.
> FARMER. Out, out upon thee, Witch !
> OLD WOMAN. Dost call me Witch ?
> FARMER. I do, Witch ; I do : and worse I would,
>   Knew I a name more hateful !

As showing how very easy it was to bring
about a conviction there is the following. It
is not by any means an isolated example, but
one picked almost at random from old trials.

The trial here was one of those emanating
from James's memorable voyage to, and from,
Oslo, already made mention of in an earlier
chapter. In this particular case the accused
was a well-educated matronly woman of Had-
dington, named Agnes Sampson. Pitcairn

in his *Criminal Trials* refers to her as " the grace wyff " or " the wyse wyff of Keith," which sufficiently shows in what manner she was respected.   The charge against her was that by means of witchcraft she had along with Johanne Feane and other witches caused such a tempest whereby the king's life was endangered ;   and there were fifty-two other counts or charges made out against her. The proceedings leading up to her arrest were that the Deputy Baillie of Tranent had in his household a half-witted maid who for some reason or other—probably because of a religious enthusiasm coupled with her half-wittedness— became suspect of witchcraft.   So the Baillie took it upon himself to question her concerning the infernal things he suspected her of having acquaintance with.   As she was stubborn, and not willing to reply to his questions, he resorted to force and applied the thumb-screw, while he searched for the witches' mark, which he eventually found on the girl's throat.   She was then put under arrest, and examined further, but not wishing to suffer unduly by not saying what was desired of her, she confessed that she was a witch, and that there were many others she could mention who were also witches.   She then glibly

named as many people as she could think of,
amongst whom was " the grace wyff," and
Johanne Feane, the schoolmaster who had
already been burned on Castle Hill.

Of course " the grace wyff " was arrested,
and put on trial, but she denied every accusation they brought against her. At first these
denials were of a gentle nature and uttered
with caution, but under the strain of the
examination she became stern and indignant.
So they shaved her head, and tied a cord
round it, and when the cord was tight they
twisted it so that the flesh was cut into ; and
then they placed over her head the witches'
bridle, a barbarous contrivance made of iron
and so fashioned that a spike having four
prongs—in shape like a quadruple fish-hook—
would be forcibly thrust into the mouth, the
prongs penetrating the palate, tongue, and
cheeks. The whole thing was then secured by
padlock. By means of a ring attached to the
collar part, the wearer could be secured to a
staple in the wall of a cell.

As though this was not enough to draw
forth confession she was forcibly kept without sleep and searched and pricked after the
manner customary with witch-hunters. And
then when courage was at zero and the mind

cared not what happened, a spurious confession of guilt was made, and of such a character as even those hardened sinners, her accusers, had never heard before, accustomed though they were to revelations of the most extraordinary description.

First of all she confessed that on All-Halloween with two hundred other witches she went to sea in a sieve and that upon returning to land at North Berwick they all went to the church there, taking hand and dancing round the pulpit; that they were then met by the Devil, who gave them all a mark—his mark—as she could testify by the one they had found on her knee. Then they rifled the vaults in the church and the graves outside the church for such things as went to the making of spells and potions. And then she had her revenge on the maid who had betrayed her by saying she was one of the company and she was the leader of a few more depraved than the rest; that she played a small harp and danced so prettily that the Devil in his enjoyment of the manner of her witchery did show his appreciation of it by thanking her afterwards in an infernal manner, together with a lot more nonsense. (It was at the trial of this maid later that the king attended in person to witness what manner of dance it was that pleased the Devil so much.) And then, perhaps hoping to flatter the king to mercy, she said she had asked the Devil why it was he hated King James so, and he had replied : " Because King James is a man of God, therefore he is my greatest enemy, and I have no power over him." But it availed her little, for witnesses came forward declaring among other things she had cured disease and sickness by charms and incantations ; that she had put a powder made out of dead men's bones under the pillow of another witch during childbirth so that her pains were transferred to someone else, and so on.

During all this time of evidence and confession it was obvious to all those around that her strength was giving out and that with every fresh accusation she became weaker and less coherent. Then, as though realising her case as hopeless, she rallied, and in a most wanton manner did continue to say all manner of absurd and ridiculous things about familiars and imps that she had had to do with ; at the same time mentioning the names of many an acquaintance as being party to them. She said that when they all went to sea in a sieve they met with a big ship named " Grace of

God," which they boarded, and then after they had feasted on everything worth taking notice of, they departed; but whipped up such a tempestuous sea as to swamp the ship, everyone aboard being drowned.

Here she related how it was that the king so very nearly got drowned when returning to Oslo. She confessed that she and the Devil were the prime movers in the business, and before the cat that was the cause of the tempest was thrown into the sea (*vide* p. 43) they had tied to its paws the knucklebones belonging to dead men; for with these bones on it was able more effectively to beat the Devil's tattoo. Also that it was baptised before it was cast overboard with a curse upon it.

A black toad, she said, had been hung up by its heels so that its venom would drip into an oyster shell, which venom was waiting to enchant the king to death so soon as some of his dirty linen could be obtained to work the spell on. Everything necessary for the spell was at hand, except the linen, and when that did arrive the king would be caused to suffer " such extraordinary paines as if he had been lying upon sharpe thornes or ends of needles."

One would think that such a recital of absurdities as these would at least have caused those that were sitting in judgment to question the sanity of the confessional, but there was neither reason, justice, nor humanity in many of those that administered the law in those bad old times. The cat-baptising, the storm-raising, and grave-robbings were all believed in ; so a verdict of guilt was more than proven ; and Agnes Sampson, the grave, matron-like, well-educated " grace wyff of Keith " was taken to Castle Hill, bound to a stake, strangled, and then burned with no one to say a word in her favour, or to recommend her weary soul to God.

Another famous trial showing the remarkable character of the evidence given and accepted was that in connection with the Lancashire witches in the seventeenth century, when as many as twenty women stood together to take their trial before the Justices, the Barons of the Exchequer, Sir James Altham and Sir Edward Bromley at the Lancaster Assizes.

The women were all associated more or less with a Coven having its headquarters at a place called Malkins Towers in Pendle Forest.

The chief witch, known as Mother Demdike, was a depraved old woman of eighty or thereabouts, with a traditional witchlike physiognomy and attire, and, with such a knowledge of the nice points on which a conviction would rest—many witches found their glory in conviction—that she took what we might consider a foolish care to supply willingly the missing links in the chain of evidence even when it seemed to be wanting in the bringing about of the correct tone of mind amongst the jury for a complete and all-vanquishing verdict.

Fortunately for herself, as well as for others, she died before the trial was finished, but this put fresh zeal in the other women for enlarging the circle awaiting sentence. Under examination they most provokingly endeavoured to transfer the charges from themselves to others with whom they had quarrelled at one time or another, and which they had not forgotten. Nor were their efforts without success, for their confessions were held as good evidence for fresh charges, and it was not long before a considerable number of the people living in their particular quarter of the county were implicated in the entanglements of perjury.

When this particular trial came to an end and eight of the women were declared " not guilty " (notwithstanding twelve were condemned to be burned) such was the prejudice of the crowd that they received the intelligence, we are told, " with great displeasure."

It would seem, after a study of the psychology of the period, that any crackbrained noodle having a dislike for a relative, a neighbour or anyone else, had only to point the finger at that luckless wight and say " Witch ! " or " Sorcerer ! " and that person's life henceforth was of little value.

Take the following as a sample of what was possible. It was recorded by Webster—having also occurred in Lancashire—twelve years after the trial just mentioned. Edmund Robinson, a wicked young scamp of a boy eleven years of age living near Clitheroe, was called upon at a trial to give evidence. He said he was gathering wild plums in Pendle Forest when to his surprise he saw a black and a white hound bounding towards him. Seeing that no one followed them, and thinking they belonged to a gentleman whom he knew as being resident in the neighbourhood, he called them to him. Just at that moment a rabbit ran out of its hole and he cried " loo !

loo ! " meaning that the dogs should follow ;
but they refused to run. For their disobedience he caught them by a string which hung
from the collars they were wearing, and tied
them up to a bush with the intention of chas-
tising them with a stick. . . . The hounds
were standing in front of him and their collars
shone like gold, so he lifted the stick, but
could not beat, for they had vanished into
thin air, and in their stead stood a little boy
and an old woman.

He also said that when the hounds were
spirited away, the old woman called him to
her and offered him a silver coin of bad money
if he would promise not to say anything about
it ; also, that he refused to do as she bade him,
but said to her " Nay ! Nay ! thou art a
witch, ha ! ha ! "

The old woman then put the bad money
back into her pocket, and from under her
apron took a horse's bridle which she shook
over the head of the little boy who had taken
the place of the black dog. Immediately she
had done this he changed into a white horse,
upon which she climbed, taking with her the
boy now giving evidence. After riding some
distance, they stopped at a big barn, where
they alighted, and then they entered a stable

where there were six or seven people tied
up like horses. They were pulling at their
halters, and as they pulled so there fell from
the manger lumps of cream, butter, mush-
rooms, porringers of milk and pieces of meat.

These phantasms and many more of a like
description having been expressed by this
boy—and believed—he was taken on the
following Sunday, in custody, round the
churches of the district during service time
so that he might have the opportunity of
"recognising" amongst the congregations
assembled any of the witches he had seen in
the stable.

He had already accused a neighbour of the
name of Dickinson, as being the old woman
who had bewitched the hounds, etc., and he
had also named another old neighbour as
having been seen by himself sitting astride a
piece of wood half-way up the chimney of
his father's house. He intensified the statement by declaring that when he called upon
her to " come down thou witch, she went the
further up until coming out at the top she
flew away on a birch broom."

Accompanying the boy on his peregrina-
tions round the churches was his father, a
mason, who, by the way, had won notoriety

some few years earlier by giving evidence
against the twenty Lancashire witches. He
doubtless knew how to make the business a
profitable one, for the wily son took good care
not to recognise any who were likely to pay
well for the oversight.

It all ended by about a score of unfortunate
people being sent to the gallows or to prison,
and the boy being looked upon as a kind of
hero in the district in which he lived.

Along with a sheer inexplicable wantonness
that prompted many a witch charge and confession, there can be no doubt but that
hallucinations of a hypochondriacal nature
also played a prominent part ; as for instance,
in the charges brought by persons against
others of good living but moody mentality,
and often of some importance in the religious
sects to which they were attached either by
faith or fancy. And, also, the repeatedly
occurring confessions on the part of apparently respectable and respected old ladies of
seventy years or so, to having been in the
habit of kicking over the traces of ladylike
decorum—so to speak—and of frequenting
witches' covens and there, under the presi-
dency of a devil, indulging in such infernal

escapades as could not possibly be found existing outside the realm of imagination.

True, the people of the witchcraft period lived nearer Nature than we in our day, and talked quite frankly, without blush or shame, of things regarding which it is customary now, and rightly so, to be mute, except in psycho-analytical circles; but that does not explain everything.

There is little doubt also but that at times hallucinations regarding witches, demons, and other suchlike trumpery assumed the form of veritable epidemics, and so all-absorbing were they that even children of tender years did not escape from their baneful influence.

At one witch-trial the conviction rested—as in that of the Pendle Forest trial—upon the fantastic evidence of a child of twelve who declared that upon falling asleep she had been visited by an old woman, a neighbour (whom, by the way, she had already recognised at the trial), and had been invited by her to take an outing. The woman, the child said, brought her daughter with her and they came riding on a broomstick. Then they all three, she added, went away together on the same broomstick[1]; the daughter in front, then the

[1] A variation of this is the fairy tale "*Mother Goose.*"

witness, then the old witch. They went away through the roof of the house, over the houses at the back of the town, and then to a village some miles off. Upon arriving there, the party came down on to a roof and then they all went down the chimney into a big room where there sat a black man and twelve women. (The mystic 13 again.) They were made very welcome, and when they had partaken of a good feed the black man filled their cups from a big can, and gave each of the women a handful of gold. She herself, she said, had not been given any money; but she had been given a lot of food and drink, etc.—And this was the kind of hallucination that hanged men and women!

Quite recently in a London morning newspaper there appeared the following account of hallucination. It is of interest here as it shows to some extent how hard old beliefs are in the dying. Had it happened years and years ago someone would have been burned as a witch for it.

THE HAUNTED CHIMNEY.

Woman's Strange Story of Weird Noises and Disappearing Monkey's Tail.

An extraordinary story was told by a well-spoken middle-aged woman who complained to the magistrate at Marylebone yesterday of unusual noises in her chimney at night, and was referred to the missionary. Speaking to a journalist later, she expressed the conviction that the house was haunted. " At night," she said, " we are awakened by extraordinary noises in the chimney, and on getting up we find our sheets and clothes burned and torn, and covered with a pink powder, while the rooms are filled with a vapour which has a most awful smell and makes you giddy." She also stated that she had seen a monkey's tail disappearing up the chimney. The noises in the chimney, she added, were like a machine at work.

In the old days it was a common belief that all animals lost their tails whenever they became bewitched. In these days of universal knowledge of the science of " psycho-analysis " the fact of the one-time existence of the belief has only to be mentioned and reason for the illusion or thought regarding a tailless monkey as well as other particularisations is obvious. " Imagination," as Shakespeare says, " sees more devils than vast hell can hold, and gives to airy nothing a local habitation and a name."

With regard to hallucinations one is reminded of a Londoner who many years ago—when other Londoners had time to spare to take notice and record such occurrences—sought protection from the Lord Mayor against " a gang of villains profoundly skilled in pneumatic chemistry " who assailed him by what he described as " an air-loom."

He gave a lengthy account of the seven persons composing the gang ; he invented names for the torments he imagined they inflicted upon him, and even made a plan of the room from where he believed them to work their spells, and also a diagram of a never-before-seen apparatus which he imagined they used.

Among other things which he believed was that they could constrict the fibre of his tongue laterally so that he could not readily speak ; that they could spread a magnetic warp beneath his brain so that the sentiments of the heart could have no communication with the operation of the intellect ; that they could at pleasure change the sense of hearing to the leg or any other part ; that by means of the air-loom and magnetic impregnations they could introduce into the brain some particular idea ; that they could violently force fluids into the head, elongate or diminish the brain, and many other things then considered to be equally absurd, but now within the range—perhaps—of serum therapy or the possibilities of wireless.

The astounding manner in which charges of witchcraft were brought against people, would indeed be amusing if it were not so tragic. For instance: In a broadsheet published in the West Countrie early in the eighteenth century there is given an account of a charge of witchcraft which was brought against the Minister of Bodmin—a Rev. Mr. Wood. It declared that "whilst the gude man was walking along a country road he was overtaken by another on horseback, who in passing cast a spell and at the same time presented the pedestrian with a strangely written document."

The report goes on to say that "the dark and hellish power of witchcraft being exercised upon him he forthwith became strangely disordered, and in a perspiring condition did gallop about a neighbour's paddock like a young colt." This might possibly have been a simple way he had of showing off some asinine quality. Still, one never knows!

However, he was arrested, and on examination, the strange document—"the spell"—was found in his waistcoat pocket. Fortunately for him, the jury were sympathetic in their verdict, and only his waistcoat was ordered to be burnt. He was declared then as having become quite rational in his behaviour.

The conduct of this last case shows that the beginning of the end was drawing nigh, and juries were no longer inclined to tolerate all the absurdities brought forward by the accusers.

Another interesting account, but with a different ending, appeared in a leaflet printed by a Mr. Hills of Blackfriars, London, also in 1704. It tells of " a notorious witch " that was discovered hiding in a garret in Water Lane. According to this Blackfriars chronicle she had certain infernal and diabolical powers which played havoc among her neighbours' children. She was in the habit, so it said, of terrifying the youngsters with apparitions of tremendous cats and causing them—the children, not the cats—to vomit pins. She was also credited with having a voice like a drill-sergeant of Kitchener's Army. So much so, indeed, it was alleged, that upon her entry into a shop and commencing to ask questions of the tradesman, all the tinned goods and chattels would fall to the ground on account of the vibration.

As a reward for her accomplishments, she

was made to take her trial before the usual
nondescript tribunal, with the result that she
was placed in a ducking-stool and dipped in
the river. There she seems to have had a
lively time, for the report quaintly adds:
" When placed under the water she popped
up again and again, and swam like a cork."
By either good or bad luck on this occasion
her life was not forfeited, but as she showed
her ingratitude by " striking a young man a
blow, from which he turned as black as coal
and died and was buried in St. Sepulchre's
Churchyard," she was therefore carried in-
gloriously to the justices at Clerkenwell,
where on the 23rd July, 1704, she was sentenced to a term of imprisonment, the exact
period of which is not mentioned.

The factor that counted for most in the
witchcrafts of these later periods was, without doubt, hallucination. Every individual
mind seemed to have its own set of beliefs
regarding witches, just as a child to-day has
its particular liking for a particular golliwog
or doll. And perhaps it would not be out
of place to mention here a few remarks on
the subject by our old friend Robert Burns,
who lived in that period when all witches

had not, according to popular opinion, entirely vanished.

"Among the many witch-stories I have heard," says he in his *Letters*, "I distinctly remember only two or three. The first, upon a stormy night, amid whistling squalls of wind and bitter blasts of hail ; in short, on such a night as the devil would choose to take an air in ; a farmer or farmer's servant was plodding and plashing homewards with his plough-irons on his shoulder, having been getting some repairs on them at a neighbouring smithy. His way lay by the kirk of Alloway, and being rather on an anxious lookout in approaching a place so well known to be a favourite haunt of the devil and the devil's friends and emissaries, he was struck aghast by discovering through the horrors of the storm and stormy night, a light, which on his near approach plainly showed itself to proceed from the haunted edifice. Whether he had been fortified from above on his devout supplication, as is customary with people when they suspect the immediate presence of Satan, or whether, according to another custom, he got courageously drunk at the smithy, I will not pretend to determine, but so it was that he ventured to go up to, nay, into the very kirk. As luck would have it, his temerity came off unpunished.

"The members of the infernal junto were all out on some midnight business or other, and he saw nothing but a kind of kettle or cauldron, depending from the roof, over the fire, simmering some heads of unchristened children, limbs of executed malefactors, etc., for the business of the night. It was in for a penny, in for a pound, with the honest ploughman; so without ceremony he unhooked the cauldron from off the fire, and, pouring out the damn'd ingredients, inverted it on his head, and carried it fairly home, where it remained long in the family, a living evidence of the truth of the story."

"Another story," Burns says, "which I can prove to be equally authentic, is as follows:— On a market day in the town of Ayr, a farmer from Carrick, and consequently whose way lay by the very gate of Alloway kirkyard in order to cross the River Doon at the old bridge, which is about two or three hundred yards farther on than the said gate, had been detained by his business, till by the time he reached Alloway it was the wizard hour, between night and morning.

"Though he was terrified with a blaze stream-ing from the kirk, yet as it is a well-known fact that to turn back on these occasions is running by far the greatest risk of mischief, he prudently advanced on the road. When he had reached the gate of the kirkyard he was surprised and entertained, through the ribs and arches of an old Gothic window, which still faces the highway, to see a dance of witches merrily footing it round their old sooty blackguard master, who was keeping them all alive with the power of his bagpipe. The farmer stopping his horse to observe them a little, could plainly descry the faces of many old women of his acquaintance and neighbour-hood. How the old gentleman was dressed tradition does not say ; but that the ladies were all in their smocks ; and one of them happening unluckily to have a smock which was considerably too short to answer all the purpose of that piece of dress, our farmer was so tickled that he involuntarily burst out with a loud laugh, ' Weel luppen, Maggy, wi' the short sark ! ' and recollecting him-self, instantly spurred his horse to the top of his speed. I need not mention the univer-sally known fact, that no diabolical power can pursue you beyond the middle of a running stream. Lucky it was for the poor farmer that the River Doon was so near, for, notwithstanding the speed of his horse, which was a good one, he reached the middle of the arch of the bridge, and consequently the middle of the stream, the pursuing, vengeful hags were so close on his heels that one of them actually made spring to seize him, but it was too late ; nothing was on her side of the stream but the horse's tail, which immediately gave way at the infernal grip, as if blasted by a stroke of lightning ; but the farmer was beyond her reach.

"However, the unsightly, tailless condition of the vigorous steed was to the last hour of the noble creature's life an awful warning to the Carrick farmers not to stay too late in the market of Ayr."

CHAPTER XIII

A TYPICAL WITCH-TRACT

FOR a hundred years after the happenings as recorded in Chapters IX and X there was a continued repetition of charges similar in character. What perhaps did more than anything else during those hundred years to keep alive the dismal business was the publicity given to it in vulgar news-sheets, street-ballads, and notorious witch-tracts. One of these rare witch-tracts has come into the possession of the writer of this book, and as the chances are that few readers have ever seen one it is reprinted in the following pages. In one or two instances, however, it has had perforce to be toned down on account of its being far too rugged in expression. This particular tract is one of the last to have been printed.[1]

[1] Some idea as to the rarity and money value of such tracts may be gathered from the fact that at the Britwell Library sale in London, in March, 1925, two of them bound together were sold for £230; while at another sale a few weeks later, thirteen tracts written by Increase Mather, the New England divine, and father of Cotton Mather, who figured so prominently in the American witchcraft persecutions, was valued as high as £900.

THE
Northamptonshire Witches.

Being a true and faithful ACCOUNT of the Births,
Educations, Lives, and Conversations,

OF

Elinor Shaw, and *Mary Phillips*,
(The two notorious Witches)

That were Executed at *Northampton* on *Saturday*,
March the 17th, 1705, for bewitching a Woman
and two Children to Death. &c.

CONTAINING

The manner and occasion of their turning Witches,
the League they made with the Devil, and the
strange Discourse they had with him ; As also
the particulars of their amazing Pranks and
remarkable Actions, both before and after their
Apprehension, and how they Bewitched several
Persons to Death, besides abundance of all sorts
of Cattle, even to the ruin of many Families,
with their full Confession to the Minister, and
last Dying Speeches at the place of Execution,
the like never before heard of.

Communicated in a Letter last Post, from Mr.
Ralph Davis, of *Northampton*, to Mr. William Simons,
Merchanttin *London*,

Licensed according to Order.

London, Printed for F. Thorn, near Fleet-street, 1705

THE

Northamptonshire Witches.

THE

Birth and Education, Lives, and Conversations, of Elinor Shaw, and Mary Phillips, &c.

SIR,

According to my Promise in my last, I have sent you here Inclosed a faithful Account of the Lives, and Conversations of the two notorious Witches, that were Executed on the Northside of our Town on Saturday the 17th instant, and indeed considering the extraordinary Methods these wicked Women used to accomplish ther Diabolical Art ; I think it may merit your Reception, and the more, since I understand you have a Frind near Fleet-street, who being a Printer, may make use of it in order to oblige the Publick ; which take as followeth, viz.

To proceed in order, I shall first begin with Ellinor Shaw (as being the most notorious of the two) who was Born at Cotterstock, within

a small Mile of Oundle in Northamptonshire,
of very obscure Parents, who not willing, or
at least not able to give their Daughter any
manner of Education ; she was left to shift
for her self at the age of 14 years, at which
time she got acquainted with a Partener in
Wickedness, one Mary Phillips, Born at
Oundle aforesaid, with whom she held a
frindly Correspondence for several Years together, and Work'd very hard in a seeming
honest way for a Livelihood ; but when she
arriv'd to the age of 21 she began to be a very
wicked Person talk'd of not only in the Town
of Cotterstock where she was Born, but at
Oundle, Glapthorn, Benefield, Southwick, and
several Parts adjacent, and that as well by
Children of four or five Years of Age, as Persons of riper Years ; so that by degrees her
Name became so famous, or rather infamous,
that she could hardly peep out of her Door,
but the Children would point at her in a Scof-
fing manner, saying, There goes a Witch,
there's Nell the Strumpet, &c. which repeated
Disgrace, agravated her Passion to such a
degree, that she Swore she would be revenged
on her Enemies, tho she pawn'd her Soul for
the Purchase. To Mary Phillips her Partener
in Knitting, who was as bad as her self in the

Vices aforesaid she then communicated her
Thoughts, relating to a Contract with the
Devil. . . . In fine, as these two agreed in their
Wickedness, to go Hand in Hand to the Devil
together for Company ; but out of a kind of
Civility, he sav'd them that Trouble for he
immediately waited upon 'em to obtain his
Booty, on Saturday the 12th of February
1704, about 12 a Clock at Night (according to
their own Confessions) appearing in the shape
of a black tall Man, at whose approach they
were very much startled at first, but taking
Ellinor Shaw by the Hand he spoke thus,
says he, be not afraid for having power given
me to bestow it on whom I please, I do assure
you, that if you will pawn your Souls to me
for only a Year and two Months, I will for all
that time assist you in whatever you desire :
Upon which he produced a little piece of
Parchment, on which by their Consents
(having prick't their Fingers ends) he wrote
the Infernal Covenant in their own Blood,
which they signed with their own Hands,
after which he told them they were now as
substantial Witches as any were in the World,
and that they had power by the assistance of
the Imps, that he would send them to do
what Mischief they pleased.

I shall not trouble you with what is already mention'd in the Tryals of these two Persons, because it is in Print by your Friend already, but only instance what was omitted in that, as not having room here to contain it altogether; but as to their general Confessions after their Condemnations take as followeth.

The Day before they were Executed Mr. Danks the Minister visited them in Prison; in order if possible to bring them to a State of Repentance, but seeing all pious Discourse prov'd inefectual; he desired them to tell him what mischeivous Pranks they had Play'd, and what private Conference they had with the Devil, from time to time, since they had made that fatal Bargain with him: To which Elinor Shaw with the Consent of the other, told him, that the Devil in the Shape of a Tall black Man appear'd several times to them, and at every Visit would present them with new Imps, some of a Red Coulour others of a Dun and the third of a black Coulour, and that these infernal Imps did Nightly visit each of them; and that by the assistance of these Animals they often Kill'd Men, Women and Children, to the great surprise of all the Towns thereabouts; she further adding that it was all the Delight they had to be doing such wicked Actions, and that they had Kil'd by their Inchantments, and Witchcraft in the space of nine Months time 15 Children, eight Men, and six Women, tho' none was suspected of being Bewitch'd but those two Children and the Woman that they Dy'd for ; and that they had Bewitch'd to Death in the same Space of Time 40 Hoggs of several poor People, besides 100 Sheep, 18 Horses, and 30 Cows, even to the utter Ruin of several Families : As to their particular Intreagues and waggish Tricks, I have not Room to enumerate they are so many, only some remarkable Feats they did in Prison, which was thus, viz. one Day Mr. Laxon and his Wife coming by the Prison, had the Curiosity to look through the Grates, and seeing of Ellinor Shaw, told her, that now the Devil had left her in the Lurch as he had done the rest of his Servants ; upon which the said Ellinor, was observ'd to Mutter strangely to her-self in an unknown Language for about two Minutes, at the end of which Mr. Laxon's Wifes Cloaths were all turn'd over her Head, Smock and all in a most strange manner, and stood so for some time at which the said Ellinor having Laughed Heartily. The Keeper of the Prison, having

one Day Threatned them with Irons, they by
their Spells caused him to Dance almost an
Hour in the Yard, to the Amazment of the
Prison, nay, such Pranks, were Play'd by
them during their Confinement, that no one
durst give them an ill Word, insomuch that
their Execution was the more hastened in the
regard of their frequent Disturbances, and
great Mischief they did in several places of
the Town, notwithstanding their Imprisonment :

They were so hardened in their Wickedness
that they Publickly boasted that their Master,
(meaning the Devil) would not suffer them to
be Executed, but on Saturday Morning being
the 17th Instant they were carried to the
Gallows on the North-side of the Town
whither numerous Crowd's of People went to
see them Die, and being come to the place of
Execution, the Minister repeated his former
pious Endeavours, to bring them to a sence of
their Sins, but to as little purpose as before ;
for instead of calling on God for Mercy,
nothing was heard from them but very bad
language : However a little before they were
ty'd up, at the request of the Minister,
Ellinor Shaw confessed not only the Crime for
which she Dyed, but openly declared before

them all how she first became a Witch, as did also Mary Phillips ; and being desired to say their Prayers, they both set up a very loud Laughter, calling for the Devil to come and help them in such a Blasphemous manner, as is not fit to Mention ; so that the Sherif seeing their presumptious Impenitence, caused them to be Executed with all the Expedition possible ; even while they were raving, and as they liv'd the Devils true Factors, so they resolutely Dyed in his Service, to the Terror all People who were eye Witnesses of their dreadful and amazing Exits.

So that being Hang'd till they were almost Dead, the Fire was put to the Straw, Faggots, and other Combustable matter, till they were Burnt to Ashes. Thus Liv'd and thus Dyed, two of the most notorious and presumptious Witches, that ever were known in this Age.

I am Sir,

Your humble Servant
RALPH DAVIS.

Northampton, March
    18th 1705

CHAPTER XIV

THE LAST PHASE

A S the reader has already been told, the general attitude towards those accused of witchcraft was changing considerably at the beginning of the eighteenth century. The people, or at least the educated and enlightened, were rather tired of the whole business, while the justices before whom charges of witchcraft had to be heard turned sympathetically towards those that were accused.

The trials themselves were less frequent than formerly, while many of those that did take place were fortunate enough to be heard before Lord Chief Justice Sir John Holt, a man of remarkable fearlessness, whose judicial career was entirely free from bias or intrigue.

Of this Sir John Holt there is an anecdote which is worth repeating. It is as follows :—
At Oxford, in his University days, he went with some other merry companions to a country inn, and there ran up a bill which

could not be met. A council of direct action
was formed by the party, with Holt as
chairman. He had observed that the innkeeper's daughter looked very ill, and so,
playing himself off as a medical student,
he asked her father what it could be that
ailed her. In reply he was informed that
she suffered from ague. Holt then gathered
together various plants, mixed them up with
great ceremony, and after rolling them up in
parchment, scrawled upon the ball a few
Greek words. The charm thus prepared he
suspended round the neck of the young
woman, and, strange to say, the ague immediately subsided. Holt, upon offering to
pay his bill—after the cure—was refused to
be allowed to do so by the grateful landlord,
and the whole party were enabled to leave
the inn, congratulating themselves, without
doubt, upon their diplomacy.

Many years afterwards, when Holt was on
the Bench, a woman was brought before him,
accused of pretending to cure disease by
means of magic and witchcraft. She admitted the charge and also confessed that she
had in her possession a ball of herbs in
parchment which she had been in the habit
of using for the cure of ague or fever.

The charm was produced and handed to the judge, who immediately recognised it as being the indentical "charm" he had prepared in his youthful frolics. The woman was acquitted. The audacity of young Holt's stratagem apparently was only equalled by the amount of faith or cure put into the charm by those who were willing. Yet this very case did more in exposing the folly of punishing too severely those accused of witchcraft than can readily be imagined.

" Charms," as everyone knows, are " as old as Adam," but possibly everyone does not know that more often than not they were invocations to the Devil. Black, in his *Folk Charms*, says that an old Devonshire woman carried about with her a charm on parchment for the curing of St. Vitus's dance. The characters on the parchment were hard to read and no one understood what they meant until a scholar interpreted them, and they were :

> " Shake her, good devil,
> Shake her once well,
> Then shake her no more
> Till you shake her in hell."

Another charm carried about by a woman at Chelsea for toothache was in a sealed packet which had never been opened until the woman's priest persuaded her to let him see it. Inside were the words :

> " Good devil, come here
> And take her for your pains."

Sir John Holt died in 1710, but we find the example he set as to the conducting of such cases as witch-trials to have been faithfully followed by his successors. In 1711 Chief Justice Powell, at the trial of a woman charged with the evil practices of witchcraft, scoffed openly in court at the fashionable absurdities of the witnesses for the prosecution, and boldly asking the clergy present upon what *they* wished to find *their* verdict of guilt—" *was it upon the indictment for conversing with the Devil in the shape of a cat— or not ?* "

Upon their replying " Yes, we find her guilty of that," he confessed his surprise, and regretted that he had not been able to prevent such a verdict, but that he would work assiduously for her pardon ; which, by the way, he eventually had the satisfaction of seeing granted to her.

Then in 1712, when Chief Justice Parker had a case before him, in which it was alleged that the accused had been nearly drowned whilst being " tested for witchcraft," he made it clear by his pronouncements at the Essex Summer Assizes that if the suspected witch had died under the ordeal he would have considered whether or not those parties concerned in her death should not be deemed guilty of wilful murder.

Apparently *executions* in England for witchcraft were now things of the past, and although it is somewhat difficult to tell exactly when the last execution did take place, we shall probably not be far out if we fix the year as 1705, when the two women mentioned in the old witchcraft tract on a previous page (278) were hanged until they were almost dead, and then burned in Northampton.

In 1735, in the reign of King George II, there was passed a curiously worded Act (see page 306) repealing the Act of James I, under the statutes of which the practice of witchcraft was an offence punishable by death (see page 170).

This Act of 1735 *did not*, as is commonly supposed, do away with the idea of anyone being able to play about with witchcraft. True, it abolished witchcraft as a punishable offence, but in addition it went out of its way to perpetuate the old ideas concerning witches, for it particularly stipulates that *any person who shall pretend to exercise any kind of Witchcraft, Sorcery, Enchantment, or conjuration shall for every such offence suffer imprisonment for the space of one year and shall in addition be put in the pillory four times.* Thus no one could practise witchcraft—they could pretend to, and get a year's imprisonment for their trouble. As severe as the punishment of a year's imprisonment appears to be, it was lenient in comparison with the punishment of King James's Act.

Under the statutes of this 1735 Act, however, few people were accused of pretending to practise witchcraft or were punished, because those trying the cases were broader-minded than their predecessors and discouraged convictions as much as they could. The privilege to punish, however, which up to the passing of the Act had been theirs, now passed to others.

The hangings had ended, the conflagrations that had exacted such terrible tribute had died down, but latent memory, like smouldering fires, had strange ways of becoming active, and when it flamed up, as assuredly it was bound to when someone raised the old cry

of " a witch, a witch ! " there were testings
and swimmings and drownings and many
more of the shameful old doings indulged in.
Mob-law had taken upon itself authority for
rough trial and cruel punishment for those
things of which the State with a sense of
humanitarianism had made up its mind to
take little further notice.

Thus the early years of the eighteenth
century were deeply scarred by the many
instances in which old men and helpless
women were made to suffer at the hands of
the mob.

The State may have been desirous, or even
anxious, that belief in witchcraft should be
generally discontinued, but unfortunately
there was no system for educating the masses
so that they might appreciate such a sense
of perfection.

That the uneducated and the ignorant did
not understand these new ideas with regard
to witchcraft is evident, or we should not have
had such accounts to reckon with as follows :—
A week or so after the passing of the 1735
Act, a shoemaker of Naseby named Kinsman
was suspected of witchcraft, but as the
Justices were lenient towards such when
charges were preferred against them, the

spiteful accusers thought it would give them greater satisfaction to keep the matter in their own hands, and apply the punishment themselves. So Kinsman was " conducted to a great pond in Kelmarsh lordship, and underwent the discipline of the ducking stool for being suspected as a wizard, and conspiring with the devil, his master, to prevent the lazy dairy woman's making good butter and cheese," etc.[1] Upwards of a thousand spectators were present. To prove the guilt of the accused, a spectator also got into the water, saying that he would be certain to sink before the wizard.[2]

Such " trials " as these were of frequent occurrence, and they could be quoted by the score. We will give particulars of just one or two more, and then pass on.

An old woman named Osborne, living at Tring, was suspected of bewitching a neighbour, because he had refused a request of hers for buttermilk. To solve his doubts he sent for a white (or harmless) witch from Northampton, who confirmed him in his belief, and the cottage where Mrs. Osborne lived was watched by rustics armed with

[1] *Northampton Mercury*, June 30, 1735.
[2] Only witches were supposed to float (see page 211).

pitchforks and staves, as a security against
spirits. No action would have been taken,
however, but that some speculators wanted
to attract a crowd together for the sake of
gain, and accordingly gave notice at the
several market towns that there would be a
ducking of witches at Longmarston on the
22nd of April, 1751. A large number of
persons collected on that day, and after a
vain attempt by the parish officers to keep
Mrs. Osborne and her husband out of their
hands, they were stripped, tied up in orthodox
fashion, and put into the water. The old
woman died from the effects of the cruelty,
and a chimney-sweep who especially dis-
tinguished himself by his brutality towards her
was afterwards executed and hung in chains.

The *Northampton Mercury* of August 1,
1785, records the fact that on " Thursday last
a poor woman named Sarah Bradshaw, of
Mear's Ashby, in this county, who was accused
by some of her neighbours of being a witch ;
in order to prove her innocence, submitted
to the ignominy of being dipped, when she
immediately sunk to the bottom of the pond,
which was deemed an incontestable proof
that she was no witch ! "

Some years after this an old woman named

Warden, living in Wellingborough, bore the reputation of being a witch. Some petty mischief happening, which was laid to her account, she was hauled down to the pond at Butlin's, then called Warren's Mill, where, in the presence of a crowd of persons, she was thrown into the water, and it is said she swam. How long she would have continued to float is doubtful, but her son, who was from home at the time of her abduction, on hearing that his mother had been taken to be ducked for a witch, said, " Witch or devil, she's my mother, and I'll have her," arrived at the Mill in time to save her. She lived some years after, but was always looked upon as a veritable witch. As late as 1860 there were persons living in Northampton who could remember having seen a woman ducked in the river on the charge of having bewitched the butter in the market.

When generation after generation for more than a thousand years has been made to understand both by the teachings of the Church and by various Witchcraft Acts that there was and still is such a thing as witchcraft—for the Act of 1735 making *the pretence* of it a punishable offence has never been repealed—it is no wonder that in some outlandish parts of this island of ours there are yet some folk who believe most explicitly in the old ideas of " evil eye," the " casting of spells," and many other of the attributes to the witchcraft of the bad old days.

If this were not so, how comes it that in December, 1924, we read in our daily paper an account of witchcraft in the South-west of England. In this particular case a small-holder was charged before the justices for assaulting his neighbour, a woman, by scratching her on the arm with a pin, and then threatening to shoot her. His excuse was that she had " ill-wished him and bewitched his pig." He had therefore tried to raise the spell by resorting to the ancient practice of drawing blood from the witch's arm with a pin. He no doubt felt very conscious that both himself and his pig were under a spell, and requested that the police should raid the woman's house and take possession of a crystal that she was said to have made use of. The magistrates tried to persuade the smallholder that there was no such thing as witchcraft, but he persisted in his belief. He was then sentenced to one month's imprisonment.

This case is interesting apart from the fact that it is " a witchcraft charge." Of course, no one is supposed to believe in witchcraft to-day, neither is anyone supposed to believe that they can suffer simply because an envious neighbour curses them in their wrath. But surely an oversensitive nature is deserving of as much consideration as the one neighbour who puts a curse upon another, and if the person accursed knows that he has no remedy at law simply because " *no one is supposed to believe in such things now*," what is he to do but to resort to the time-honoured expedient of " bleeding the witch " for raising the spell?—a method that for hundreds of years has been recognised as effectual even when bell, book, and candle have failed.

The fact that a crystal figures in the case is certainly suggestive of an indictable offence under the Act of 1735, in which it is stated " that if any person shall pretend to exercise or use any kind of Witchcraft, Sorcery, Enchantment, or conjuration or undertake to tell Fortunes," etc., unless of course there was no " *pretending*." A case of witchcraft coming to the front at the present time is of tremendous interest, as it raises the whole question as to whether such cases should be adjudicated upon by magistrates or treated by mental specialists.

The amount of superstition and belief that entered into witchcraft has always been tremendous, and the manner in which super stition acted on belief, and belief acted on conduct is really deserving of more considera- tion than it has yet received in so far as it is connected not only with witchcraft but with much other strange behaviour of our own time. Take, for instance, that in connection with spiritualism and certain forms of faith- healing.

That any person should believe a spell has been put upon them, or their pig, or for that matter on anyone or anything else, and should then fall into a decline and waste away as so many did in the olden days simply because of a belief in the possibility of bewitchment, or the power of the evil eye, or because they had knowledge of a fortune-teller with a crystal, or a reputed witch being in possession of a small model of wax representing them and were " torturing " it with pins, or wasting it in front of a slow fire, so that as it was pricked and wasted they felt the pain and wasted also, is, after all, not so strange a malady as at first sight it might appear to be. In a previous page it has been shown how it is possible even to die, not from disease or accident, but by simply accommodating the mind to the wished-for or dreaded condition. One may perhaps smile that so seemingly ludicrous a belief as that associated with witchcraft should get so strong a hold on the popular imagination ; but we must remember that we to-day have beliefs regarding other things that are just as absurd.

Take that connected with sea-serpents. Following time-honoured habit, we hear of him regularly every year from some seaside resort. True, it is mostly from " the other side," but we hear of him all the same. A Michigan newspaper that came to hand in August, 1924, describes in a most graphic manner the terror of bathers when they saw the monster rolling shorewards, " its huge head rising several feet out of the water, its barrel-like coils turning and twisting into view and glistening in the glaring sunlight as though coated with polished metal." Eye-witnesses declared that it " gushed thick streams of water from its cavernous mouth and distended nostrils. That its eyes were as big as soup plates ; its teeth, of which it displayed four rows, were as long and sharp as the tines of a pickaxe ; and its tail had two prongs, each about eight feet long." This is not the outcome of a fevered imagination but the product of a sane and temperate press existing not in the Middle Ages but in the year of learning 1924. And in the land of prohibition, too !

The truth is that the witches and even those who so explicitly believed in witchcraft as to allow themselves to suffer on account of it, were afflicted with mentality that was below the normal and were therefore, perhaps, more to be pitied than blamed. What was wanted more than anything else for the treatment of witchcraft was " common sense," and this did not make itself apparent until the eighteenth century ; and after, so it has been estimated, more than 30,000 women and men in England alone had paid the extreme penalty.

And again, it is quite possible that many of the " witches " were no witches at all, inasmuch as they were victims of circumstances ; poor, and often found in reputed bad company, simple and withal comparatively harmless ; and it must not be forgotten that in those red-letter days of witchcraft, witch-hunting, and witch-trials, the social condition of the majority of the people was such as to generate a scowling disposition towards kings, overlords, and priests, and whilst the possible good intentions of the one were misunderstood those of the others were despised. All mistrusted each other and numbers of disgruntled men and women sought relaxation in the excitements associated with the practice of witchcraft, much in the same way as folk of our own day and generation, suffering from mere ennui, have accepted wholeheartedly the mysticisms and the witchery of spiritualists or of psychoanalysts. Also, it must be remembered, the outbreaks of witchcraft for the most part were epidemic in character and coincident with social, political, or religious turmoil. That such should have been the case ought not to be surprising to students of sociology, who are all psychologists more or less; but it seems to have escaped their notice, for up to now all writers seem totally to have ignored it; and when we recollect the long course of ages which have by turns witnessed the reigns of magic, divination, invocations, talismans, astrology, sorcery, necromancy, enchantments, incubi, succubi, vampires, ghosts, vampirism, evil eye, werewolves, and a hundred other things described by terms of varying character and value, how can we be surprised that at times we find in our midst those whom we can describe in no other way but as " mental throwbacks " ?

And so, within the recesses of the mind, the old ideas live on, and they never fail to express themselves in a variety of ways at some time or another of life's many phases. If it were not so, and if we were not a people steeped in superstitious belief, how is it that to-day so many people wear amulets and lucky charms in the shape of black cats, lucky pigs, swastikas, and numerous other relics of a barbarous past ?

One word more : although throughout this book the beliefs and practices of the witches for the most part have been subjected to the recognised up-to-date psycho-analytical tests, the writer has purposely refrained from giving the resultant interpretations in what has come to be known as " the usual psycho-analytical way," as, apart from objections that would certainly come from those not altogether conversant with psycho-analytical expressions, it is unnecessary ; the inner meaning or psychological explanation of much of the

witches' ritual being at once only too obvious
to all intellectual readers having but the
slightest knowledge of psycho-analytical
axioms.

Readers must, therefore, to some extent—
so far as this account of witchcraft is concerned—make their own analysis ; remembering that much of the behaviour of the witches
up to about the sixteenth century was but
the expression of impulses and emotions of
primitive origin and therefore with a self-
preservative or procreative bias. Not for-
getting that, as has been mentioned already
in the opening chapter, witchcraft had its
real inception in a period of fear, wonder, and
sacrifice common to all primitives, that it
passed through the long centuries in an ever-
changing order of observance and behaviour,
and that the change was not always for the
better. The witchcraft of the third century
and earlier was very different from the
witchcraft of the twelfth century, and that
of the thirteenth to the eighteenth changed
successively with the centuries through
which it passed.

APPENDIX

As it is thought that many readers who have cared to follow the fortunes, or the misfortunes, of the witches through this book would be interested in reading the Act of 1735 (p. 306), together with that part or parts of the 1824 Act, having, or supposed to have, special reference to witchcraft (p. 311), they have been included overleaf.

THE WITCHCRAFT ACT OF 1735

ANNO REGNI

GEORGII II.

REGIS

Magnæ Britanniæ, Franciæ, & Hiberniæ,

NONO

At the Parliament begun and holden at *Westminster,* the Fourteenth Day of *January, Anno Dom.* 1734, in the Eighth Year of the Reign of our Sovereign Lord GEORGE the Second, by the Grace of God, of *Great Britain, France,* and *Ireland,* King, Defender of the Faith, &c.

And from thence continued by several Prorogations to the Fifteenth Day of *January,* 1735; being the Second Session of this present Parliament.

An Act to repeal the Statute made in the First Year of the Reign of King *James* the First, intituled, *An Act against Conjuration, Witchcraft, and dealing with evil and wicked Spirits,* except so much thereof as repeals an Act of the Fifth Year of the Reign of Queen *Elizabeth, Against Conjurations, Inchantments, and Witchcrafts,* and to repeal an Act passed in the Parliament of *Scotland* in the Ninth Parliament of Queen *Mary,* intituled, *Anentis Witchcrafts,* and for punishing such Persons as pretend to exercise or use any kind of Witchcraft, Sorcery, Inchantment, or Conjuration.

BE it enacted by the King's most Excellent Majesty, by and with the Advice and Consent of the Lords Spiritual and Temporal, and Commons, in this present Parliament assembled, and by the Authority of the same, That the Statute made in the First Year of the Reign of King *James* the First, intituled, *An Act against Conjuration, Witchcraft, and dealing with evil and wicked Spirits,* shall, from the Twenty-fourth Day of *June* next, be repealed and utterly void, and of none effect (except so much thereof as repeals the Statute made in the Fifth Year of the Reign of Queen *Elizabeth*) intituled, *An Act against Conjurations, Inchantments, and Witchcrafts.*

And be it further enacted by the Authority aforesaid, That from and after the said Twenty-fourth Day of *June,* the Act passed in the Parliament of *Scotland,* in the Ninth Parliament of Queen *Mary,* intituled, *Anentis Witchcrafts,* shall be, and is hereby repealed.

And be it further enacted, That from and after the said Twenty-fourth Day of *June,* no Prosecution, Suit, or Proceeding, shall be commenced or carried on against any Person or Persons for Witchcraft, Sorcery, Inchantment, or Conjuration, or for charging another with any such Offence, in any Court whatsoever in *Great Britain*.

And for the more effectual preventing and punishing of any Pretences to such Arts or Powers as are before mentioned, whereby ignorant Persons are frequently deluded and defrauded ; be it further enacted by the Authority aforesaid, That if any Person shall, from and after the said Twenty-fourth Day of *June*, pretend to exercise or use any kind of Witchcraft, Sorcery, Inchantment, or Conjuration, or undertake to tell Fortunes, or pretend, from his or her Skill or Knowledge in any occult or crafty Science, to discover where or in what manner any Goods or Chattels, supposed to have been stolen or lost, may be found, every Person, so offending, being thereof lawfully convicted on Indictment or Information in that part of *Great Britain* called *England*, or on Indictment or Libel in that part of Great Britain called *Scotland*, shall, for every such Offence, suffer Imprisonment by the Space of one whole Year without Bail or Mainprize, and once in every Quarter of the said Year, in some Market Town of the proper County, upon the Market Day, there stand openly on the Pillory by the Space of One Hour, and also shall (if the Court by which such Judgment shall be given shall think fit) be obliged to give Sureties for his or her good Behaviour, in such Sum, and for such Time, as the said Court shall judge proper according to the Circumstances of the Offence, and in such case shall be further imprisoned until such Sureties be given.

NINETY-ODD years after the passing of the witchcraft Act of 1735 there came into force a new Act, passed ostensibly for the purpose of making " *further provision for the suppression of vagrancy and for the punishment of idle and disorderly persons, rogues and vagabonds* " ; due to the distress in England following the Napoleonic Wars ; and the flocking to the towns of people from the rural districts in search of employment ; it has come to be known as " The Rogues and Vagabonds Act." Its connection with witchcraft is that it contains a clause as follows—" *Every person pretending or professing to tell fortunes, or using any subtle craft, means, or devices by palmistry or otherwise . . . shall on conviction be kept to hard labour for three months.*" This may in reality have nothing to do with witchcraft, but a number of people interpret the words " any subtle craft " as though it does. Under this Act, however, numerous prosecutions for fortune-telling, and so on, take place. That there is some connection between the misdemeanours of those who are convicted under it and the practices of the witches prosecuted under the Act of 1735, and its predecessor, that of James I, is undeniable. Following is a newspaper report of a 1924 case which may serve to illustrate what is meant.

A clairvoyant was at Brighton Police Court fined 40s. for " professing to tell fortunes to deceive and impose on certain of his Majesty's subjects," whilst a friend of the clairvoyant was fined 40s. for aiding and abetting. Both pleaded not guilty. The wife of a Brighton detective, who, acting as a police agent, sat for " a reading," said she was told that her husband would be very successful in a new venture which he proposed to make. The clairvoyant said she saw spirit forms and heard messages from spirits.[1]

[1] The indictment under James's Act was "dealings with familiar spirits."

THE ROGUES AND VAGABONDS ACT

ANNO QUINTO
GEORGII IV. REGIS
CAP. LXXXIII.

An Act for the Punishment of idle and disorderly Persons, and Rogues and Vagabonds, in that Part of *Great Britain* called *England*.

[21st *June* 1824.]

WHEREAS an Act was passed in the Third Year of the Reign of His present Majesty, intituled *An Act for consolidating into one Act and amending the Laws relating to idle and disorderly Persons, Rogues, and Vagabonds, incorrigible Rogues and other Vagrants, in* England : And whereas the said Act was to continue in force until the First Day of *September* One thousand eight hundred and twenty-four, and no longer ; and it is expedient to make further Provision for the Suppression of Vagrancy, and for the Punishment of idle and disorderly Persons, Rogues, and Vagabonds, and incorrigible Rogues, in *England*, etc.

IV. And be it further enacted, That every Person committing any of the Offences herein-before mentioned, after having been convicted as an idle and disorderly Person ; every Person pretending or professing to tell Fortunes, or using any subtle Craft, Means, or Device, by Palmistry or otherwise, to deceive and impose on any of His Majesty's Subjects ; every Person wandering abroad and lodging in any Barn or Outhouse, or in any deserted or unoccupied Building, or in the open Air, or under a Tent, or in any Cart or Waggon, not having any visible Means of Subsistence, and not giving a good Account of himself or herself, shall be deemed a Rogue and Vagabond, within the true Intent and Meaning of this Act ; and it shall be lawful for any Justice of the Peace to commit such Offender (being thereof convicted before him by the Confession of such Offender, or by the Evidence on Oath of One or more credible Witness or Witnesses) to the House of Correction, there to be kept to hard Labour for any Time not exceeding Three Calendar Months :

And be it further enacted, That it shall be lawful for any Person whatsoever to apprehend any Person who shall be found offending against this Act, and forthwith to take and convey him or her before some Justice of the Peace, to be dealt with in such Manner as is herein-before directed, or to deliver him or her to any Constable or other Peace Officer of the Place where he or she shall have been apprehended, to be so taken and conveyed as aforesaid ; and in case any Constable or other Peace Officer shall refuse or wilfully neglect to take such Offender into his Custody, and to take and convey him or her before some Justice of the Peace, or shall not use his best Endeavours to apprehend and to convey before some Justice of the Peace any Person that he shall find offending against this Act, it shall be deemed a Neglect of Duty in such Constable or other Peace Officer, and he shall on Conviction be punished in such Manner as is herein-after directed.

And be it further enacted, That when any incorrigible Rogue shall have been committed to the House of Correction, there to remain until the next General or Quarter Sessions, it shall be lawful for the Justices of the Peace there assembled to examine into the Circumstances of the Case, and to order, if they think fit, that such Offender be further imprisoned in the House of Correction, and be there kept to hard Labour for any Time not exceeding One Year from the Time of making such Order, and to order further, if they think fit, that such Offender (not being a Female) be punished by Whipping, at such Time during his Imprisonment, and at such Place within their Jurisdiction, as according to the Nature of the Offence they in their Discretion shall deem to be expedient.

And be it further enacted, That no Proceeding to be had before any Justice or Justices of the Peace under the Provisions of this Act shall be quashed for Want of Form, etc.

A S nothing whatsoever is said in the Act of 1824 with regard to a previous Act being annulled and made void, it would appear that the Act of 1735 is still the Law. The interpretation of the words " any subtle craft " in the 1824 Act, although thought by many to mean witchcraft, possibly doesn't mean that at all. The idea that it *does* is evidently a widely possessed one, however, or His Majesty's Stationery Office would not have supplied the writer of this book with the 1824 Rogues and Vagabonds Act when asked to be supplied with " the last Act printed dealing with witches and witchcraft " !

So it is still quite possible, or at least possible according to how the words are interpreted, " to *pretend* to exercise any kind of witchcraft . . ."— to be prosecuted under the Act of 1735 and " suffer imprisonment by the space of one whole year," or prosecuted under the Act of 1824 for " using any subtle Craft . . . to deceive . . ." or for " pretending or professing to tell fortunes " [1] to be " kept to hard labour for any time not exceeding three calendar months " for the first offence, with the addition of whippings and a prolongation of imprisonment for further offences.

But, thank goodness, legal decisions are more important than statutes, and the mere fact that so me of the provisions of the Acts have not been put into force for many years invalidates them.

[1] Under certain conditions this would apply to spiritualists: see *Times* Law Reports, May 13–14, 1925.

INDEX

315